John Harrison Tenney

Songs of Joy

A Collection of Hymns and Tunes Especially Adapted for Prayer, Praise, and Camp Meetings, Revivals, Christian Associations, and Family Worship

John Harrison Tenney

Songs of Joy

A Collection of Hymns and Tunes Especially Adapted for Prayer, Praise, and Camp Meetings, Revivals, Christian Associations, and Family Worship

ISBN/EAN: 9783337289782

Printed in Europe, USA, Canada, Australia, Japan

Cover: Foto ©Thomas Meinert / pixelio.de

More available books at **www.hansebooks.com**

A COLLECTION OF HYMNS AND TUNES,

ESPECIALLY ADAPTED FOR

PRAYER, PRAISE, AND CAMP MEETINGS, REVIVALS, CHRISTIAN ASSOCIATIONS, AND FAMILY WORSHIP.

BY

J. H. TENNEY.

AUTHOR OF "GOLDEN SUNBEAMS," "ANTHEM OFFERING," ETC.

BOSTON:
LEE & SHEPARD, PUBLISHERS.
NEW YORK:
LEE, SHEPARD & DILLINGHAM.
1875.

PREFACE.

This little collection of hymns and tunes has been prepared to meet the constantly increasing demand for Sacred Social Songs, especially adapted for Prayer, Praise, and Camp Meetings, Revivals, Christian Associations, and Family Worship.

It is not a collection of new, untried material,—"words and music written expressly for this work,"—but a collection of hymns and tunes, three-fourths of which are selected from the *choicest gems* of the most popular composers of social music in the country. Many of them are known and sung in every village in the land, where the voice of prayer, and the song of praise are heard.

The new pieces have been selected with great care, and none are inserted that will not, in our judgment, stand the test of trial.

A choice selection of the old familiar tunes, which are sung in every prayer meeting in the land, are inserted near the close of the book. Among them will be found many of Dr. Lowell Mason's most popular tunes, without which, no collection of music for social worship is complete. These tunes are used by permission of Messrs. Oliver Ditson & Co., to whom we return sincere thanks.

We gratefully acknowledge our indebtedness to Messrs. S. Brainard's Sons, John Church & Co., Benham & Stedman, A. H. Redford, W. F. Schneider, Rev. R. Lowry, D. F. Hodges, Asa Hull, W. G. Fischer, E. Roberts, and J. H. Rosecrans, for permission to use many of their most valuable copyrights; and to Messrs. P. P. Bliss, J. R. Murray, Jas. McGranahan, J. H. Leslie, O. W. Pillsbury, and Dr. J. B. Herbert, for valuable original contributions.

J. H. TENNEY.

BOSTON, *Jan. 1st*, 1875.

Entered, according to Act of Congress, in the year 1874, by J. H. TENNEY, in the Office of the Librarian of Congress, at Washington.

SONGS OF JOY.

JOYFUL BE THE HOURS TO-DAY.

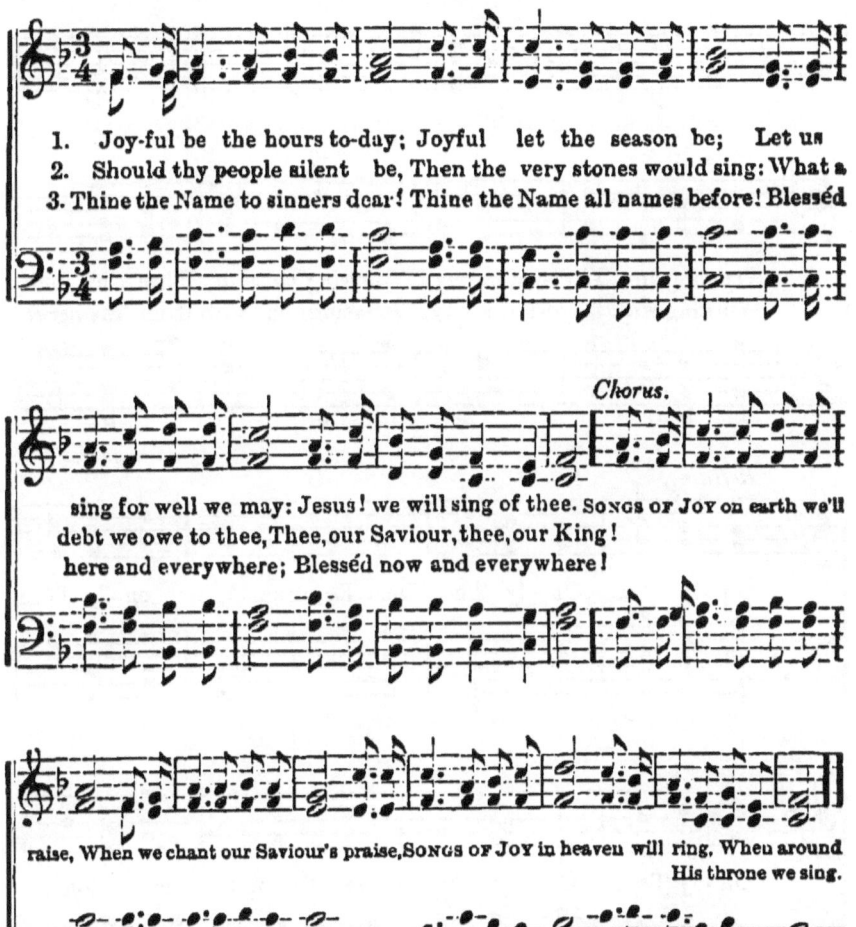

4 ONLY THEE.

REV. S. WOLCOTT, D.D. J. H. TENNEY.

From "Golden Sunbeams," by per.

1. Dear Redeemer, on-ly Thee Would my waiting spir-it own,
   Trusting in Thy sym-pa-thy, Clinging close to Thee a-lone.
2. Gracious Master, on-ly Thee Would my willing spir-it serve,
   Working with fi-del-i-ty, Pressing on with dauntless nerve.

Refrain.
On-ly Thee, On-ly Thee, Dear Re-deem-er, on-ly Thee,
On-ly Thee, On-ly Thee; Close I'll cling to Thee a-lone.

3.
Blest Immanuel, only Thee
 Would my longing spirit claim,
Yearning for Thy purity,
 Glowing with love's quenchless [flame.

4.
Lord of glory, only Thee
 Would my loving spirit praise,
Off'ring grateful melody,
 Waking glad immortal lays.

"IT IS I!"

E. A. WALKER. J. H. TENNEY.

1. "It is I!" O blessed Jesus! Speak to me that cheering word;
   High above the foaming billows, Let its gentle sound be heard;
   For the sea of grief o'erwhelms me, And my spirit faints thro' fear;
   And I long to hear those accents, Telling me that thou art near.

2. "It is I!" How blest the token To the stranger in the wild!
   Desolate I am no longer, Feel no more an orphan child.
   "It is I!" Those words shall guide me To my Father's house above,
   Where I face to face shall see thee, Whom not having seen, I love.

3.
"It is I!" That voice shall soften
 All the anguish of my pain,
Be my strength in utmost weakness,
 In my deepest grief sustain.
Never shall a cloud o'erspread me,
 Wrapping me in darkness round;
But its gloom shall flee most surely
 At the music of that sound.

4.
"It is I!" O Jesus! speak it [brow;
 When the death-dew damps my
Let me hear thee softly whisper,
 "I am with thee even now."
Then no more shall death affright me,
 Knowing thee, my Saviour, nigh;
Feeling infinite compassion
 In the blessed "It is I!"

3.
A stranger here, I pitch my tent
  Beneath this spreading tree:
Here shall my pilgrim life be spent:
  No home like this for me!
  No home like this for me, &c.

4.
For burden'd ones a resting-place,
  Beside that cross I see;
I here cast off my weariness:
  No rest like this for me!
  No rest like this for me, &c.

THE VALLEY OF BLESSING. 7

Annie Wittenmyer.   Wm. G. Fischer. By per.

1. I have entered the valley of blessing so sweet, And Jesus abides with me there;
2. There is peace in the valley of blessing so sweet, And plenty the land doth impart;

And his spirit and blood make my cleansing complete, And his perfect love casteth out fear.
And there's rest for the weary worn traveler's feet, And joy for the sorrowing heart.

Chorus.

O come to this valley of blessing so sweet, Where Jesus will fulness bestow—
Oh, believe, and receive, and confess him, That all his salvation may know.

3. There is love in the valley of blessing so sweet,
Such as none but the blood-washed may feel;
When heaven comes down redeemed spirits to greet,
And Christ sets his covenant seal.—*Chorus.*

4. There's a song in the valley of blessing so sweet,
That angels would fain join the strain,
As, with rapturous praises, we bow at his feet,
Crying, "Worthy the Lamb that was slain."—*Chorus*

NEARER HOME.

From "Golden Sunbeams," by per.
J. H. Tenney.

NEARER HOME. Concluded.

3.
Worn and weary, oft the pilgrim
  Hails the setting of the sun,
For the goal is one day nearer,
  And his journey nearly done.
Thus we feel, when o'er life's desert,
  Heart and sandal worn we roam,
As the twilight gathers o'er us,
  We are one day nearer home.

4.
Nearer home! yes, one day nearer
  To our Father's house on high,
To the green fields and the fountains
  Of the land beyond the sky.
For the heav'ns grow brighter o'er us,
  And the lamps hang in the dome,
And our tents are pitch'd still closer,
  For we're one day nearer home.

DRESDEN.

FANNY CROSBY.   E. ROBERTS, by permission.

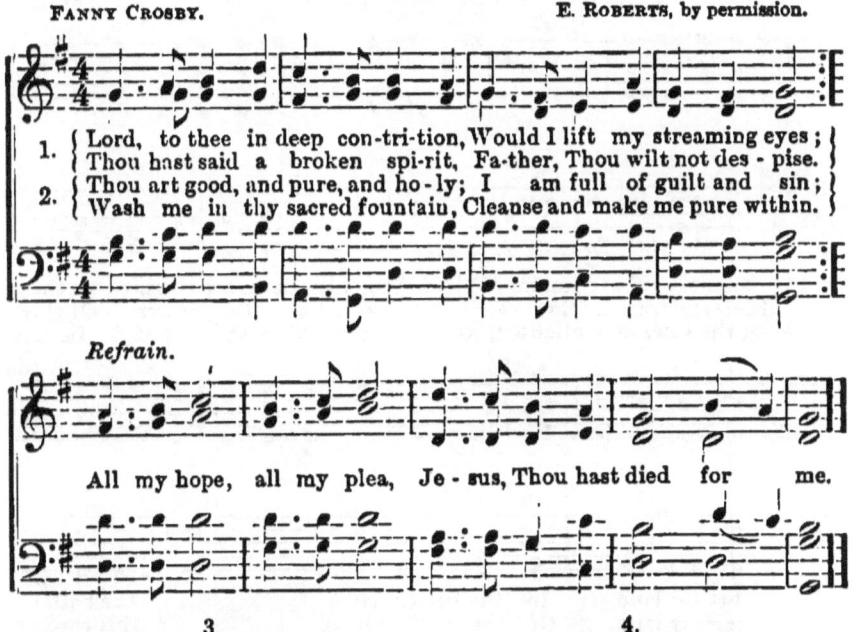

3.
Let thy healing beams of mercy,
  Drop, for me, one cheering ray,
Father, from thy gracious presence,
  Cast, oh, cast me not away.
    Refrain.—All my hope, &c.

4.
Lord, forgive me, own and bless me,
  I am weak, but thou art strong;
In the path of heavenly wisdom,
  Gently lead my soul along.
    Refrain.—All my hope, &c.

THE PILGRIM'S SONG.

DR. H. BONAR.   J. H. TENNEY.

1. A few more years shall roll, A few more seasons come;
And we shall be with those that rest, Asleep within the tomb:
Then, O my Lord, prepare My soul for that great day;
Oh, wash me in thy precious blood, And take my sins away!

2. A few more storms shall beat, On this wild, rocky shore;
And we shall be where tempests cease, And surges swell no more:
Then, O my Lord, prepare My soul for that calm day;
Oh, wash me in thy precious blood, And take my sins away!

3.
A few more struggles here,
  A few more partings o'er,
A few more toils, a few more tears,
  And we shall weep no more:
Then, O my Lord, prepare,
  My soul for that blest day;
Oh, wash me in thy precious blood,
  And take my sins away!

4.
A few more Sabbaths here
  Shall cheer us on our way;
And we shall reach the endless rest,
  Th' eternal Sabbath-day:
Then, O my Lord, prepare
  My soul for that sweet day;
Oh, wash me in thy precious blood,
  And take my sins away!

14   I AM WAITING BY THE RIVER.

W. O. CUSHING.   J. H. TENNEY.

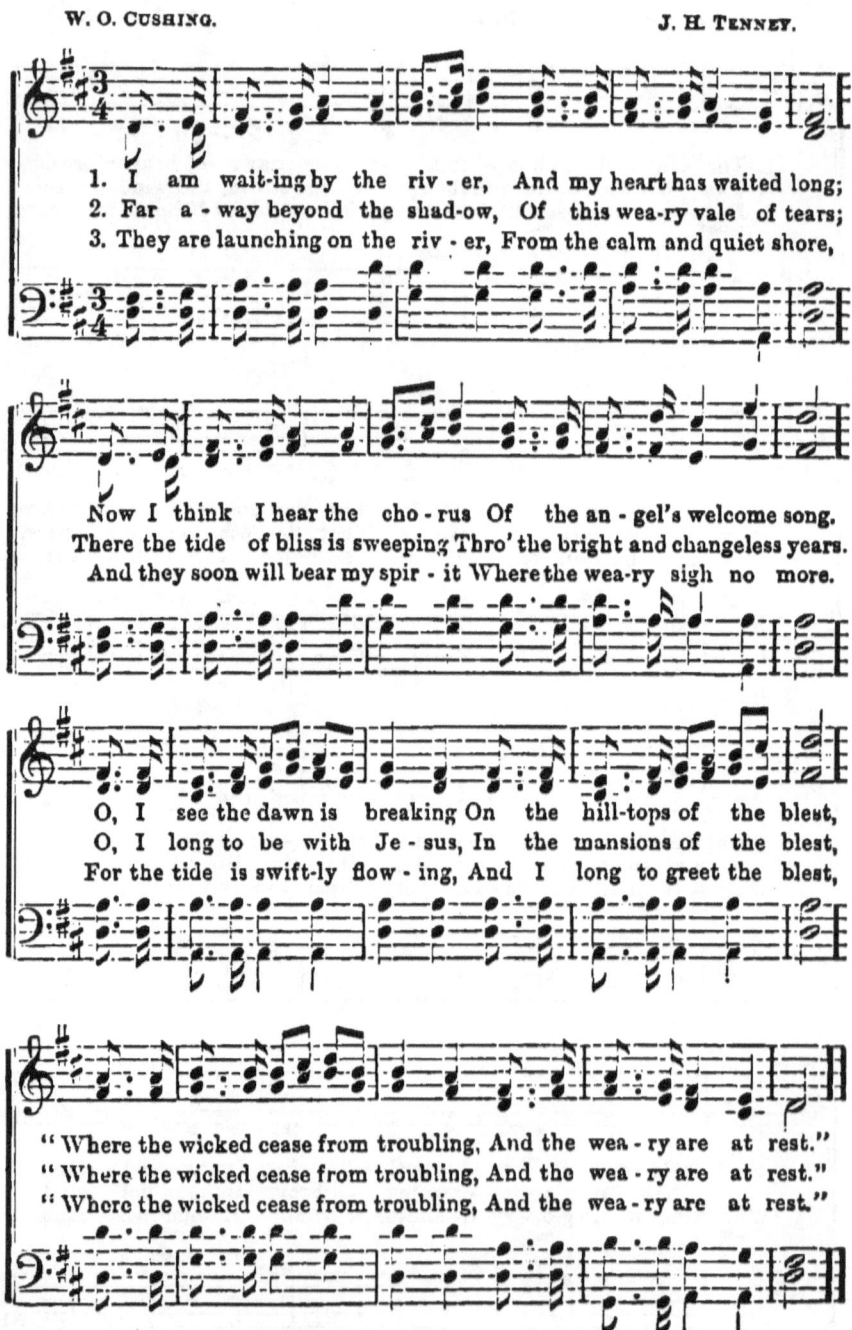

1. I am wait-ing by the riv - er, And my heart has waited long;
2. Far a - way beyond the shad-ow, Of this wea-ry vale of tears;
3. They are launching on the riv - er, From the calm and quiet shore,

Now I think I hear the cho - rus Of the an - gel's welcome song.
There the tide of bliss is sweeping Thro' the bright and changeless years.
And they soon will bear my spir - it Where the wea-ry sigh no more.

O, I see the dawn is breaking On the hill-tops of the blest,
O, I long to be with Je - sus, In the mansions of the blest,
For the tide is swift-ly flow - ing, And I long to greet the blest,

"Where the wicked cease from troubling, And the wea - ry are at rest."
"Where the wicked cease from troubling, And the wea - ry are at rest."
"Where the wicked cease from troubling, And the wea - ry are at rest."

I LOVE TO TELL THE STORY.—Concluded. 21

glo - ry, To tell the old, old sto-ry, Of Je-sus and his love.

NEARER, MY GOD, TO THEE.

From "Golden Sunbeams," by per.

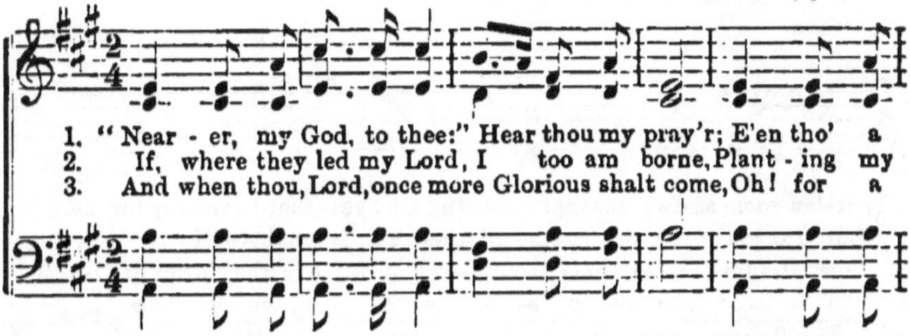

1. "Near - er, my God, to thee;" Hear thou my pray'r; E'en tho' a
2. If, where they led my Lord, I too am borne, Plant - ing my
3. And when thou, Lord, once more Glorious shalt come, Oh! for a

heav - y cross Faint-ing I bear; Still all my pray'r shall be,
steps in His, Wea - ry and worn; May the path car - ry me
dwell - ing place, In thy bright home! Thro' all e - ter - ni - ty,

Near - er, my God, to thee: Nearer, my God, to thee; Nearer to thee!
Near - er, my God, to thee; Nearer, my God, to thee; Nearer to thee!
Near - er, my God, to thee; Nearer, my God, to thee; Nearer to thee!

THERE'S ROOM FOR ALL.

JOSEPHINE POLLARD. From "The Tonart," by per. E. ROBERTS.

1. In those beautiful mansions of glo-ry, Whose wonders I'm longing to see,
2. Oh, I fear I shall never be worthy Such holy communion to share;
3. Oh, I'm glad, yes, I'm glad that a Saviour, To perishing sinners was given;

There's a room and a place that is waiting, Oh! yes, that is waiting for me.
But I'll pray ev'ry day to my Father, To fit me to dwell with Him there.
For His love and His pity secured me A share in the glories of Heaven.

Chorus.

Yes, Oh! yes, there is room, Room for all in heaven; In those beau-ti-ful mansions of glo - ry, There's room, there's room for all.

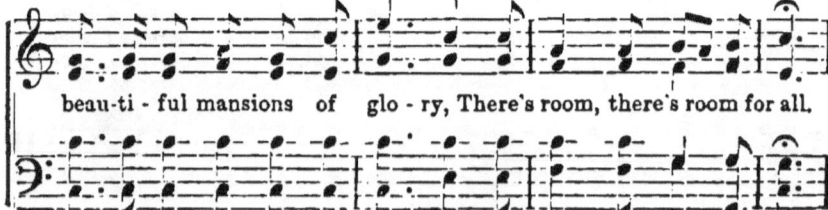

HARK! 'TIS THE WATCHMAN'S CRY. 23

O. W. PILLSBURY.

TUNE,—" There's room for all," page 22.

4. 'Tis the thought that sustains me in trial,
    And comforts when burdened with care,—
  There is rest and a refuge in heaven,
    And oh! there is room for me there.—CHO.

5. Not a sigh nor a groan shall escape us,
    No tear-drops of sorrow shall fall ;
  There's a peace and a joy that's eternal,
    In heav'n—and there's room for us all.—CHO.

3.
That meeting, O how sweetly dear!
What sounds shall greet the list'ning ear!
What thrills of rapture wake the soul,
As back those golden gates shall roll,
  Beyond the swelling flood!

4.
Dear Saviour! guide my willing feet;
That I may have that joy complete;
And live to praise thro' endless day
The love that dries all tears away,
  Beyond the swelling flood!

BEAUTIFUL RIVER.

Words and Music by Rev. R. Lowry, by per.

1. Shall we gather at the riv-er, Where bright angel feet have trod:
2. On the mar-gin of the riv-er, Washing up its sil-ver spray,

With its crys-tal tide for-ev-er Flowing by the throne of God?
We will walk and worship ev-er, All the hap-py, gold-en day.

Chorus.

Yes, we'll gather at the riv-er, The beautiful, the beautiful riv-er—

Gather with the saints at the riv-er That flows by the throne of God.

3.
On the bosom of the river,
Where the Saviour-king we own,
We shall meet and sorrow never
'Neath the glory of the throne.
Cho.

4.
Ere we reach the shining river,
Lay we every burden down;
Grace our spirits will deliver,
And provide a robe and crown.
Cho.

5.
At the smiling of the river,
Rippling with the Saviour's face,
Saints, whom death will never sever,
Lift their songs of saving grace.
Cho.

6.
Soon we'll reach the shining river,
Soon our pilgrimage will cease;
Soon our happy hearts will quiver
With the melody of peace.
Cho.

28 JESUS IS MIGHTY TO SAVE.

Mrs. Annie Wittenmyer. Wm. G. Fischer, by per.

1. All glo-ry to Je-sus be giv'n, That life and sal-va-tion are free;
2. From the darkness of sin and despair, Out in-to the light of his love,
3. Oh, the rapturous heights of his love, The measureless depths of his grace;
4. In him all my wants are supplied, His love makes my heaven below,

And all may be wash'd and forgiv'n, And Jesus can save e-ven me.
He has bro't me and made me an heir, To kingdoms and mansions above.
My soul all his fulness would prove, And live in his loving em-brace.
And freely his blood is applied, His blood that makes whiter than snow.

Chorus. migh-ty to save,
Yes, Je-sus is migh-ty, is migh-ty to save, And

may know
all his sal-va-tion, sal-va-tion may know, On his bosom I lean, And his

JESUS IS MIGHTY TO SAVE. Concluded. 29

HE CALLETH THEE.

GRACE WEBSTER HINSDALE.   From "Golden Sunbeams," by per.   D. F. HODGES.

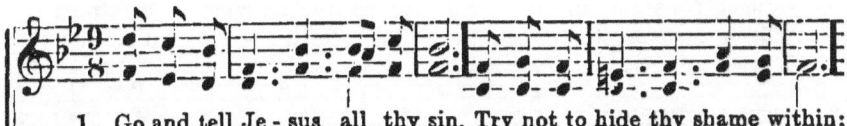

1. Go and tell Je-sus all thy sin, Try not to hide thy shame within;
2. Go and tell Je-sus thou art lost; Think of the price thy ransom cost;
3. How canst thou doubt thy waiting Lord? Where is thy faith in Jesus' word?

Go and tell Je-sus all thy fears, Trust thou his love, he knows thy tears!
Think of his cross, think of his prayer, Hear his kind voice, do not despair.
O, cease to wound that loving breast, Where all thy hopes of life must rest.

Refrain.

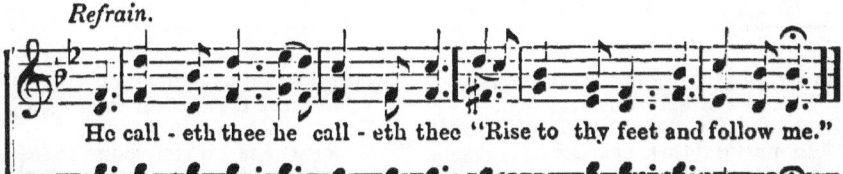

He call-eth thee he call-eth thee "Rise to thy feet and follow me."

THE HALLOWED SPOT.

From "Golden Sunbeams," by per.

1. There is a spot to me more dear Than native vale or mountain; A spot for which affection's tear Springs from its grateful fountain: 'Tis not where kindred souls abound, Tho' that is almost heav-en, But where I first my Saviour found, And felt my sins for-giv-en.

2. Hard was my toil to reach the shore, Long toss'd upon the o-cean; A-bove me was the thunder's roar, Beneath, the waves' com-mo-tion; Dark-ly the pall of night was thrown Around me, faint with terror; In that dark hour how did my groan Ascend for years of er-ror.

3.
Sinking and panting for my breath,
  I knew not help was near me:
And cried, O save me, Lord, from death,
  Immortal Jesus, hear me!
Then quick as thought, I felt him mine,
  My Saviour stood before me,
I saw his brightness round me shine,
  And shouted, Glory! Glory!

4.
O sacred hour! O hallow'd spot!
  Where love divine first found me;
Wherever falls my distant lot,
  My heart shall linger round thee.
And when from earth I rise to soar
  Up to my home in heaven,
Down will I cast my eyes once more,
  Where I was first forgiven.

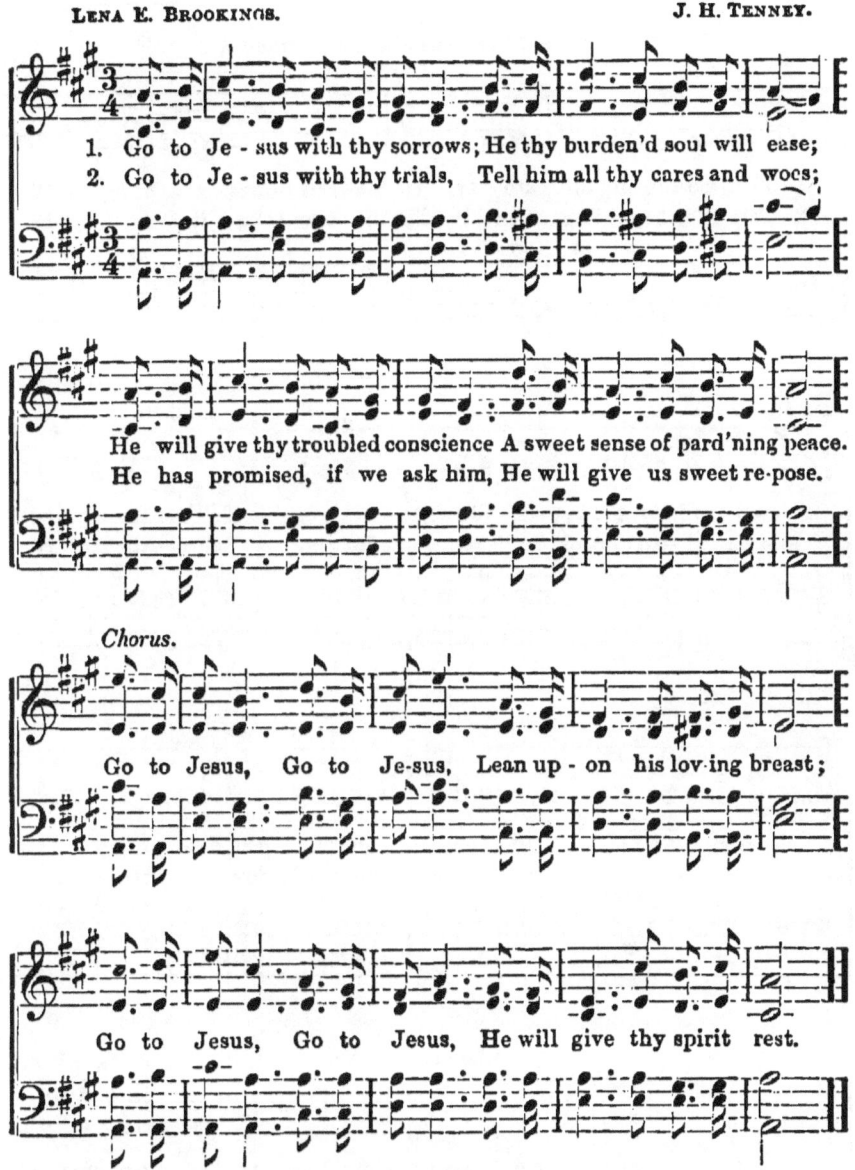

3.
Go to Jesus when thy burdens
  Are too hard for thee to bear;
Tell him all thy cares and sorrows,
  He will lend a list'ning ear.

4.
Go to Jesus when death's shadows
  Quickly gather round thy way;
Ask of him to guide thy footsteps
  To the realms of endless day.

THE OLD, OLD STORY. Concluded.

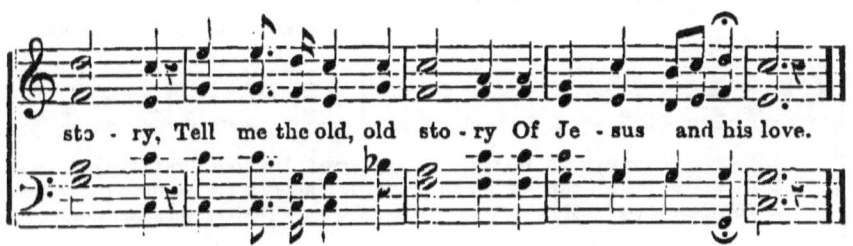

sto-ry, Tell me the old, old sto-ry Of Je-sus and his love.

3.
Tell me the story softly,
  With earnest tones, and grave;
Remember! I'm the sinner
  Whom Jesus came to save.
Tell me that story always,
  If you would really be,
In any time of trouble,
  A comforter to me.

4.
Tell me the same old story,
  When you have cause to fear
That this world's empty glory
  Is costing me too dear.
Yes, and when that world's glory
  Is drawing on my soul,
Tell me the old, old story:
  "Christ Jesus makes thee whole."

GOING HOME.

Popular Melody.

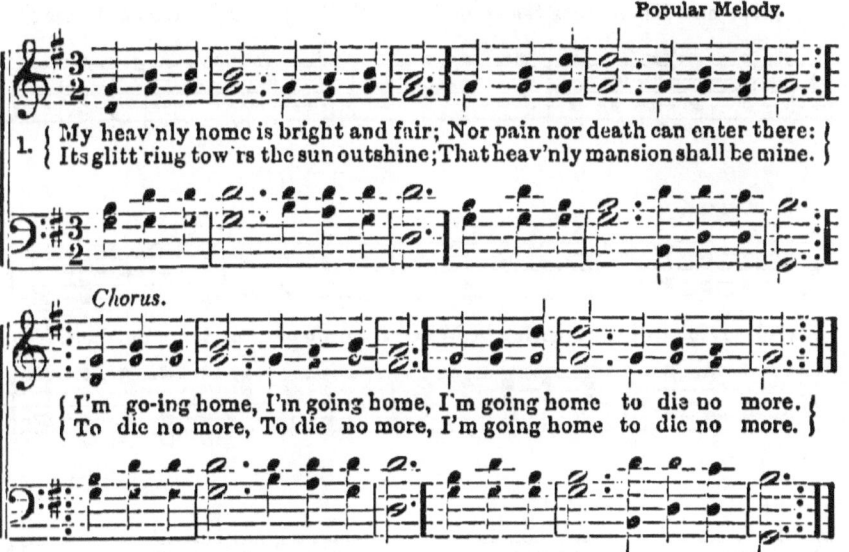

1. { My heav'nly home is bright and fair; Nor pain nor death can enter there:
     Its glitt'ring tow'rs the sun outshine; That heav'nly mansion shall be mine. }

Chorus.

{ I'm go-ing home, I'm going home, I'm going home to die no more.
  To die no more, To die no more, I'm going home to die no more. }

2. My Father's house is built on high,
   Far, far above the starry sky;
   When from this earthly prison free,
   That heavenly mansion mine shall be.—Cho.

3. Let others seek a home below,
   Which flames devour, or waves o'erflow;
   Be mine a happier lot to own,
   A heavenly mansion near the throne.—Cho.

BEHOLD THE LAMB OF GOD.

"And they crucified him."—MARK xv. 25.   J. H. TENNEY.

1. The gen-tle, ho-ly Je-sus, Without a spot or stain, By wick-ed hands was ta-ken, And cru-ci-fied and slain.
2. His hands and feet are pierc-ed; He can-not hide his face; And cru-el men stand gaz-ing, In crowds a-bout the place.
3. For you and me he suffered: 'Twas for our sins he died; And not for our sins on-ly, But all the world's be-side!

Chorus.
Look, look,—if you can bear it, Look at your dy-ing Lord! Stand near the cross, and watch Him; "Behold the Lamb of God!"

4.
And now the work is "finished,"
The sinner's debt is paid,
Because on Christ the righteous,
The sin of all was laid.

5.
Ah wonderful redemption!
God's remedy for sin;
The door of heaven is open,
And you may enter in.

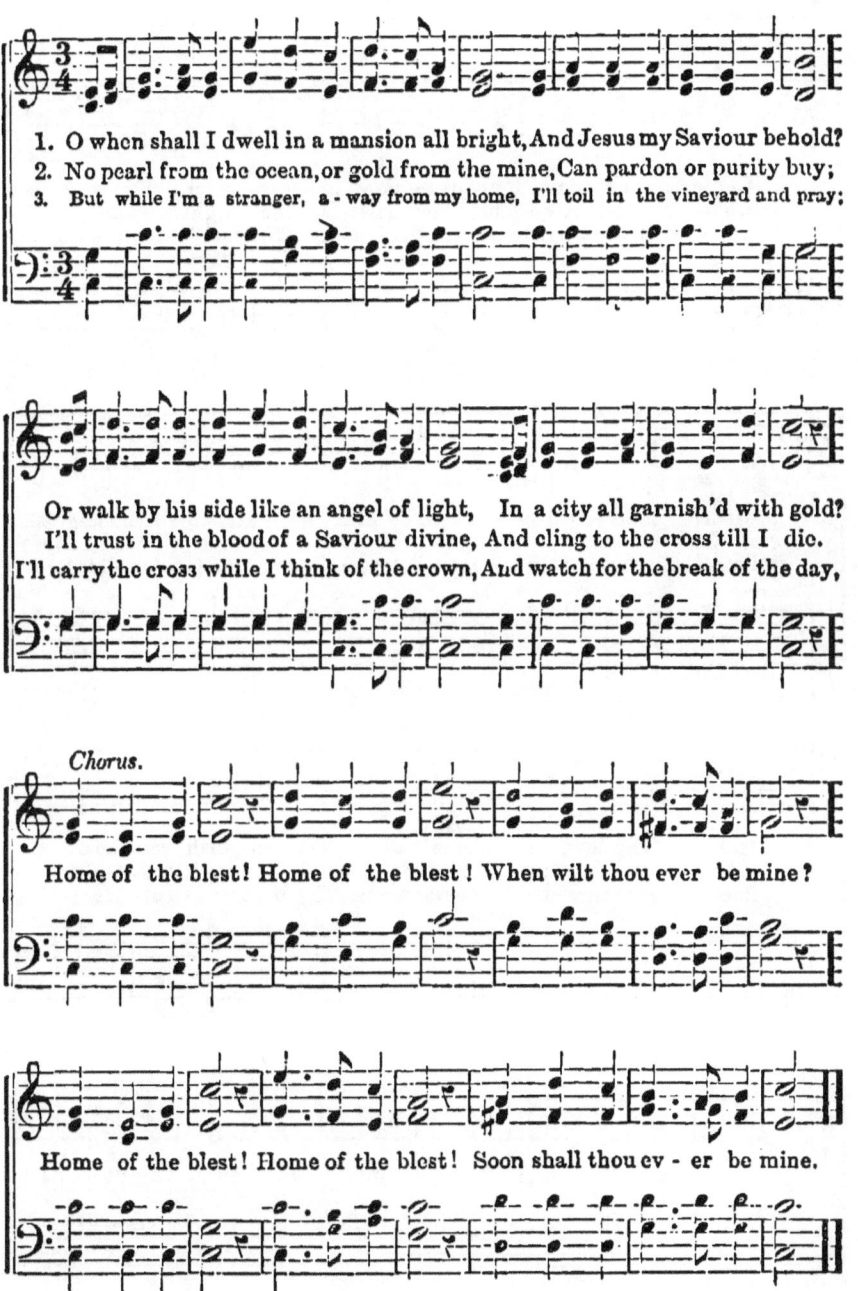

38 COME TO ME, SAVIOUR.

From "The Pearl," by per. of S. BRAINARD'S SONS, Cleveland, O.

M. P. A. CROZIER. FRANK M. DAVIS.

Tenderly.

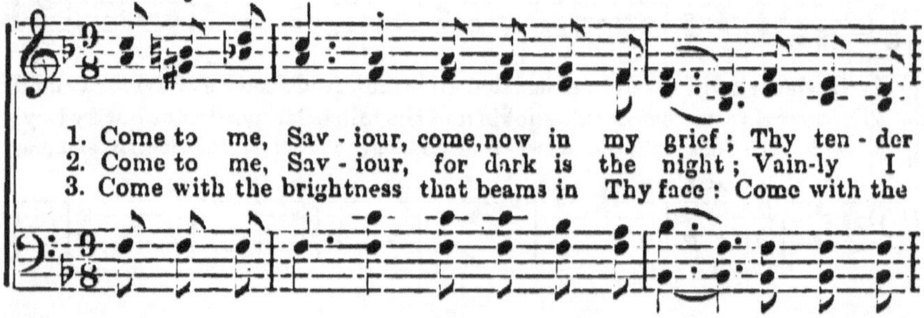

1. Come to me, Sav-iour, come, now in my grief; Thy ten-der
2. Come to me, Sav-iour, for dark is the night; Vain-ly I
3. Come with the brightness that beams in Thy face: Come with the

presence is sweetest re-lief; Thy heart hath known all the anguish I
seek for some star's feeble light; O-pen my eyes to be-hold at my
smiles of Thy mercy and grace; Come, and with footsteps as silent and

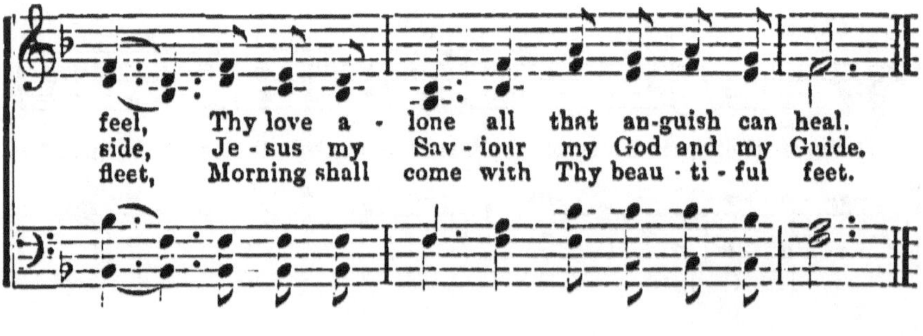

feel, Thy love a-lone all that an-guish can heal.
side, Je-sus my Sav-iour my God and my Guide.
fleet, Morning shall come with Thy beau-ti-ful feet.

Chorus.

Come to me, Sav-iour, Come to me, Sav-iour, Thy heart hath

COME TO THE SAVIOUR. Concluded.

MIDST SORROW AND CARE.

2.
'Tis Jesus, our friend,
On whom we depend,
For life and all its rich blessings.

3.
When trouble assails,
His love never fails,
He meets us with rich consolation.

OVER THERE.

41

From "Golden Sunbeams," by per.   J. H. TENNEY.

1. There's a band of an-gel watchers, Just a-cross the foaming tide,—
2. Wait - ing there with smiling faces, In their robes of spotless white;

O - ver by the dark cold wa - ters, Waiting on the oth-er side.
While far out upon the riv - er, Comes to us a gleam of light.

Chorus.
Hark! there's music on the wa - ters, Borne a - long the balmy air,
An - gel voices ringing, ring - ing, "Over there, just over there!"

3.
O'er our earthly homes are gathered,
Many a shadow, many a gloom,
For the loved ones who are sleeping,
In the silence of the tomb.

4.
But these scenes will soon be over :
Soon we'll join the angel band;
Soon we'll clasp the forms that bind us,
To the unseen spirit land.

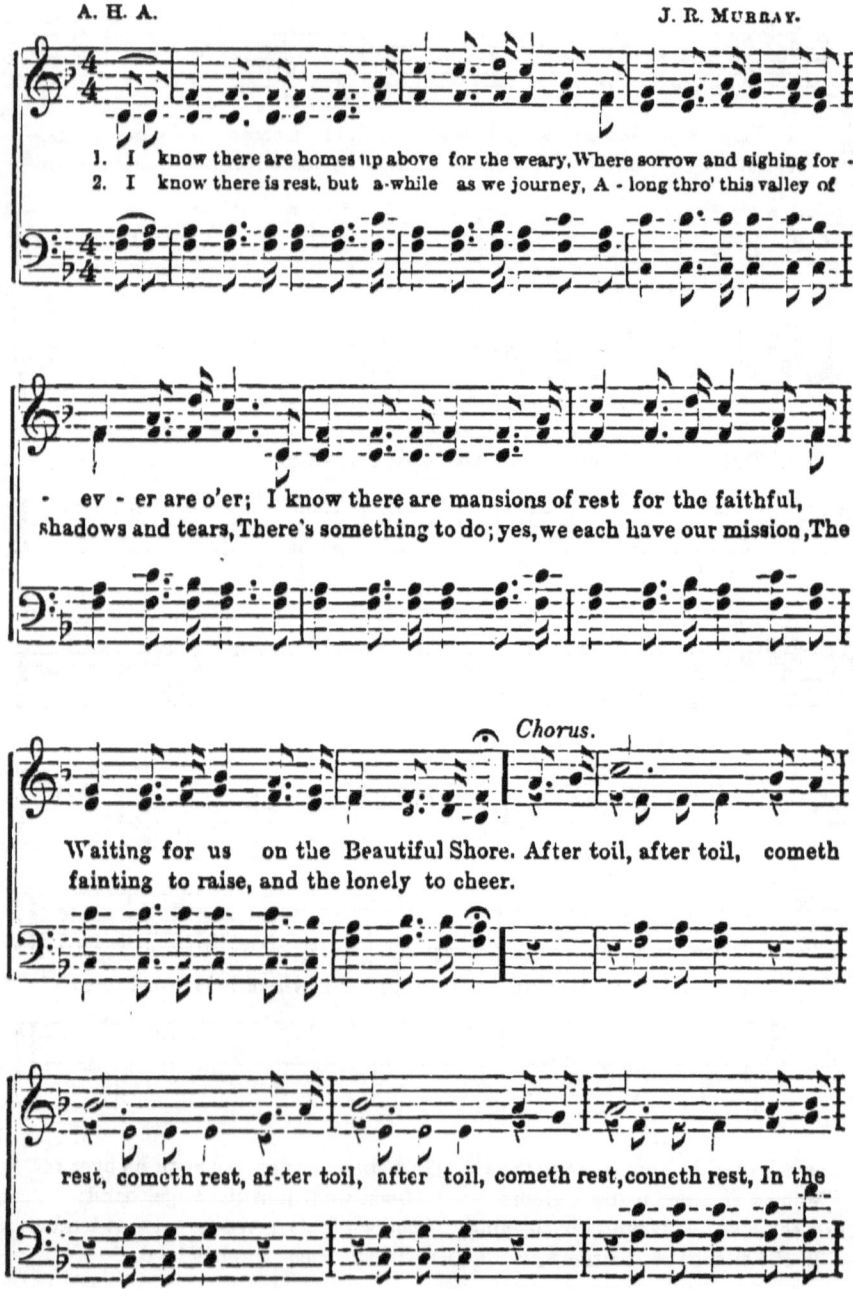

AFTER TOIL COMETH REST. Concluded.

sweet, sweet home of the good and blest, After toil, after toil cometh rest.

3. Let us make them to feel that this earth's not all sadness,
    That dark clouds have linings of silver and gold,
    And point them to Jesus, their loving Redeemer,
    Whose love and affection can never be told.
        CHO.—After toil, &c.

4. Then let us not linger in sighs, and grow weary,
    Remember the rest that is waiting above,
    For those who have finished their mission, believing,
    That Jesus was leading them home by his love.
        CHO.—After toil, &c.

COME UNTO ME.

From "Golden Sunbeams," by per.

1. Come unto me, when shadows darkly gather, When the sad heart is
2. Large are the mansions in thy Father's dwelling, Glad are the homes that
3. There, like an E-den blos-som-ing in glad-ness, Bloom the fair flow'rs the

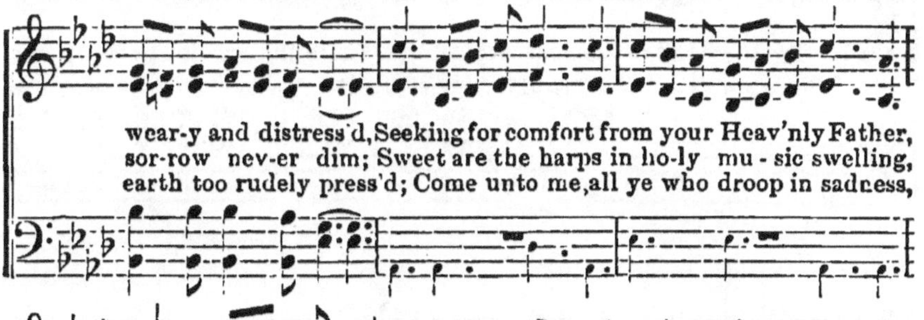

wear-y and distress'd, Seeking for comfort from your Heav'nly Father,
sor-row nev-er dim; Sweet are the harps in ho-ly mu-sic swelling,
earth too rudely press'd; Come unto me, all ye who droop in sadness,

Come un-to me, and I will give you rest.
Soft are the tones that raise the heav'n-ly hymn.
Come un-to me, and I will give you rest.

44 SHALL WE KNOW EACH OTHER?

REV. R. LOWRY, by per.

SHALL WE KNOW? &c. Concluded.

3.
Yes, my earth-worn soul rejoices,
  And my weary heart grows light,
For the thrilling angel voices,
  And the angel faces bright,
That shall welcome us in heaven,
  Are the loved of long ago,
And to them 'tis kindly given
  Thus their mortal friends to know.

4.
Oh! ye weary, sad, and toss'd ones,
  Droop not, faint not by the way;
Ye shall join the lov'd and just ones,
  In the land of perfect day!
Harpstrings touched by angel fingers,
  Murmured in my raptured ear,
Evermore their sweet song lingers,
  "We shall know each other there!"

TO-DAY.
J. H. T.

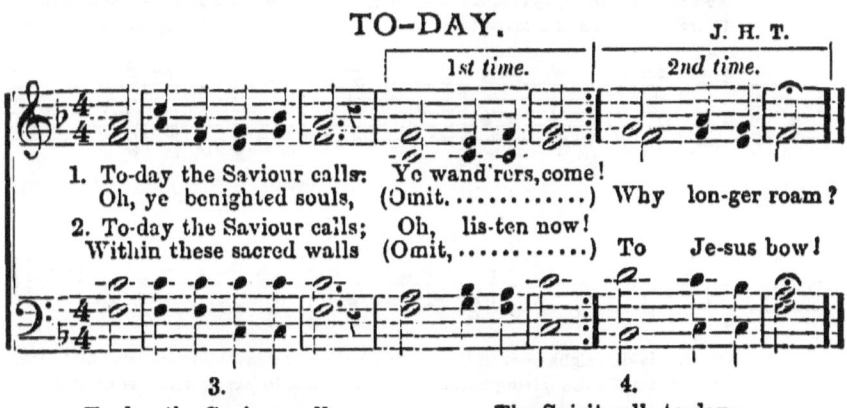

3.
To-day the Saviour calls;
  For refuge fly;
The storm of justice falls,
  And death is nigh.

4.
The Spirit calls to-day;
  Yield to his power;
Oh, grieve him not away!
  'Tis mercy's hour.

WHO WILL GATHER THE GRAIN ? 47

THE SUNNY SHORE. Concluded.

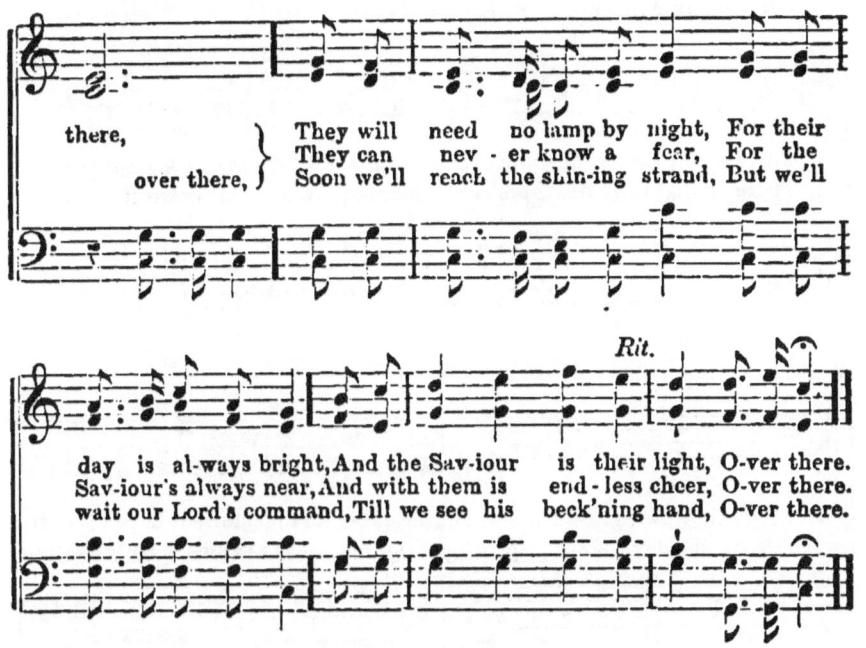

COME UNTO ME.

LIGHTS ALONG THE SHORE. Concluded. 51

love of Jesus' name, And they guide us, yes they guide us un-to him.

3.
O they tell of a hope that will cheer us
In the midst of our sorrows and cares,
When the lamp on our vessel burns
  dimly,
We watch for the glimmer of their's.

4.
Then forgot not to keep your light shin-
  ing ;
O Christian, be earnest and true,
For a soul on life's ocean may perish,
May sink in the waves but for you.

PERRIN. C. M.

J. H. TENNEY.

1. There is a safe and se-cret place, Beneath the wings divine, Reserved for all the
2. He feeds in pastures large and fair, Of love and truth di-vine ; O child of God, O
3. A hand al-mighty to de-fend, An ear for eve-ry call, An honored life, a

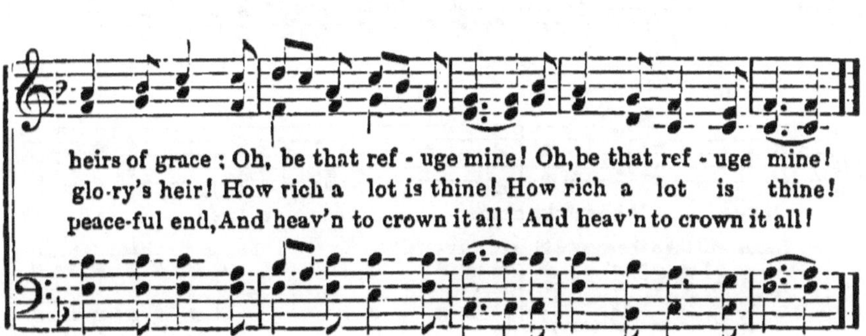

heirs of grace ; Oh, be that ref - uge mine! Oh, be that ref - uge mine!
glo-ry's heir! How rich a lot is thine! How rich a lot is thine!
peace-ful end, And heav'n to crown it all! And heav'n to crown it all!

52. THE VOICE OF MERCY.

Mrs. E. C. ELLSWORTH. J. H. TENNEY.

1. Sinner so thoughtless, change thy way, Turn to the Saviour, turn to-day,
2. Sinner despondent, why delay, Come to the Saviour, come to-day,
3. Sinner so hardened, wilt thou fear? Day of his wrath shall soon appear,

Death follows hard, then quickly flee, Flee to the refuge made for thee.
Mer-cy he gives thee, freely gives; Then why despair, since Jesus lives!
Can'st thou endure the judgment-day, Without that Friend, the Christian's stay?

Chorus.

Sinner be wise........ O come, O come........ Jesus will take...... thee safely home; Sinner give heed...... O flee, O
Sinner be wise, O come to Jesus, come to-day, Jesus will take thee, yes, will take thee safely home: Sinner give heed, O flee to

THE VOICE OF MERCY. Concluded.

flee,...... Lest sin be - guile........ and ru - in thee.
Jesus while you may,   Lest sin beguile and ru - in thee.

THY WILL BE DONE.

BENJAMIN SCHMOLK. J. H. TENNEY.

1. My Je-sus, as thou wilt! Oh, may thy will be mine! In-to thy hand of
2. My Je-sus, as thou wilt! Tho' seen thro' many a tear, Let not my star of
3. My Je-sus, as thou wilt! All shall be well for me: Each changing future

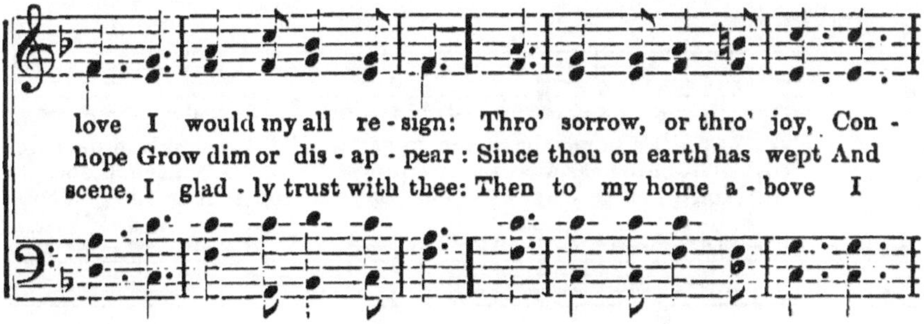

love I would my all re - sign: Thro' sorrow, or thro' joy, Con -
hope Grow dim or dis - ap - pear : Since thou on earth has wept And
scene, I glad - ly trust with thee: Then to my home a - bove I

- duct me as thine own, And help me still to say, My Lord, thy will be done!
sorrowed oft a-lone, If I must weep with thee, My Lord, thy will be done!
trav - el calmly on, And sing, in life or death, My Lord, thy will be done!

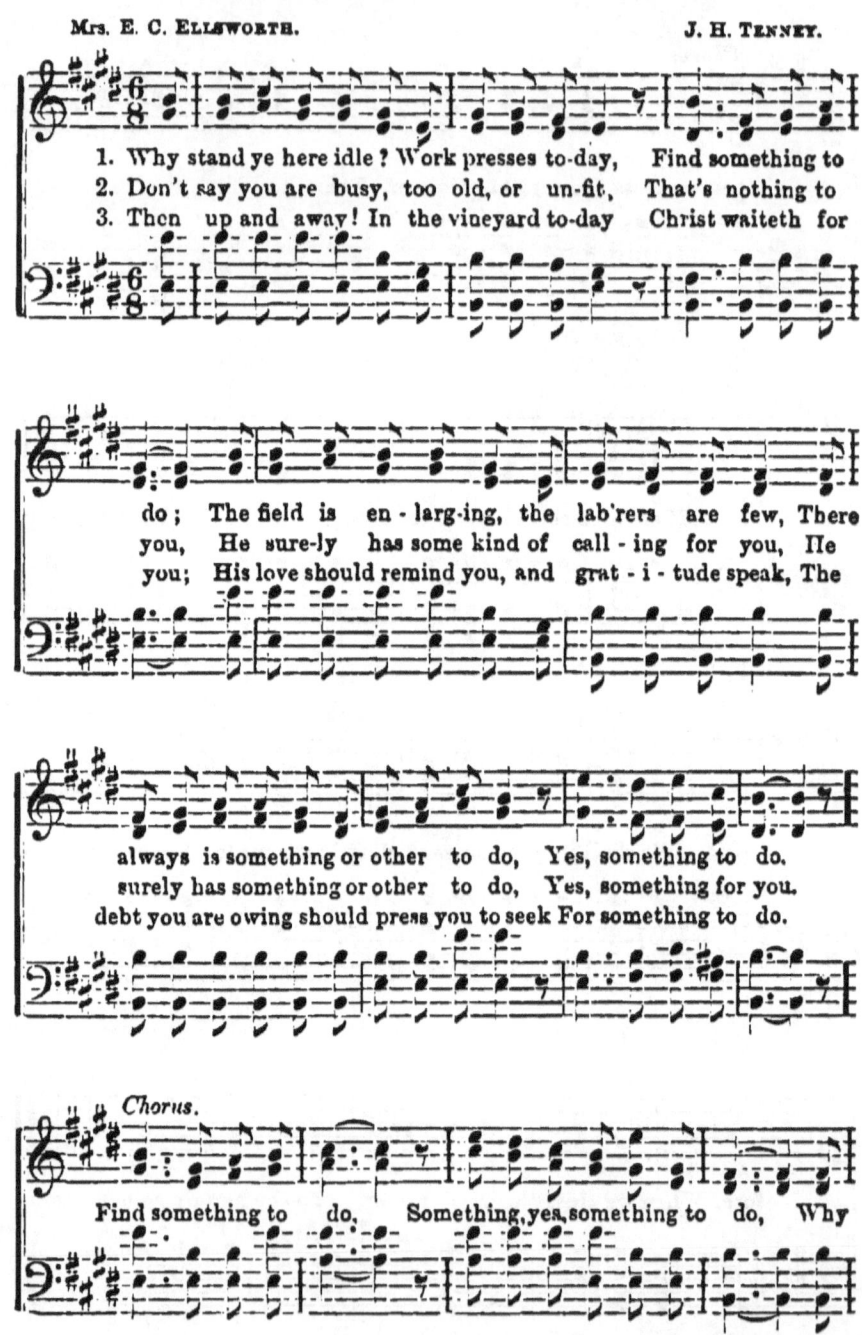

THERE'S SOMETHING TO DO. Concluded.

stand ye here idle? work presses to-day, Find something, yes, something to do.

JEHOVAH JIREH.
(THE LORD WILL PROVIDE.)

Mrs. M. A. W. Cook.   J. H. Tenney.

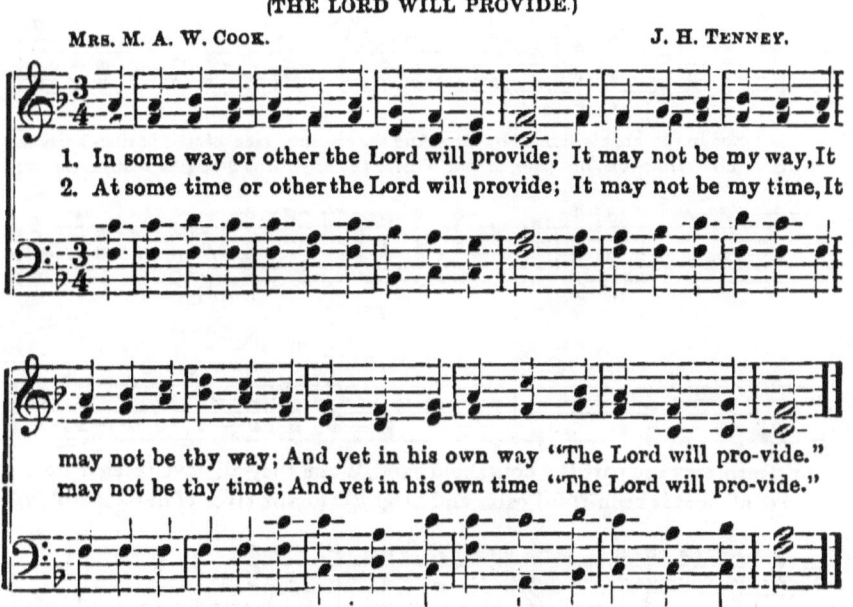

1. In some way or other the Lord will provide; It may not be my way, It
2. At some time or other the Lord will provide; It may not be my time, It

may not be thy way; And yet in his own way "The Lord will pro-vide."
may not be thy time; And yet in his own time "The Lord will pro-vide."

3. Despond, then, no longer; the Lord will provide;
    And this be the token,
    No word He hath spoken,
    Hath ever been broken,
  "The Lord will provide."

4. March on, then, right boldly; the sea shall divide;
    With Canaan before us,
    With Heaven's mercy o'er us;
    We'll join in the chorus,
  "The Lord will provide."

EVEN ME.

J. H. TENNEY.

4.
Pass me not, O mighty Spirit!
Thou canst make the blind to see;
Witnesses of Jesus' merit!
Speak some word of pow'r to me.
           Cho.

5.
Love of God so pure and changeless;
Blood of Christ—so rich, so free;
Grace of God—so strong and boundless,
Magnify it all in me!
           Cho.

KEEP ON PRAYING. Concluded. 61

Keep on praying to the end, Keep on praying to the end;
Cheer up, brother, keep on pray-ing, Keep on praying to the end.

WILL YOU GO?

Western Melody.

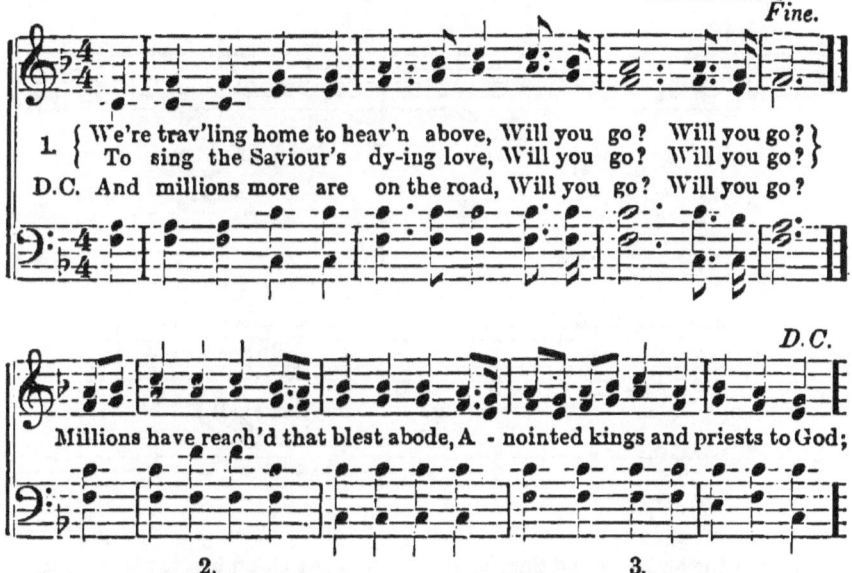

1. We're trav'ling home to heav'n above, Will you go? Will you go?
To sing the Saviour's dy-ing love, Will you go? Will you go?
D.C. And millions more are on the road, Will you go? Will you go?

Millions have reach'd that blest abode, A-nointed kings and priests to God;

2.
We're going to walk the plains of light;
  Will you go?
Far, far from curse and death and night;
  Will you go?
The crown of life we then shall wear,
The conqueror's palm we then shall bear,
And all the joys of heaven we'll share;
  Will you go?

3.
The way to heaven is straight and plain;
  Will you go?
Repent, believe, be born again;
  Will you go?
The Saviour cries aloud to thee,
"Take up your cross and follow me,
And thou shalt my salvation see."
  Will you go?

THE LAND CELESTIAL.

FANNY CHURCH.
From "The Little Sower," by per.
J. H. ROSECRANS.

1. There is a land ce-les-tial, A world that's bright and fair;
There flows the peace-ful riv-er, Be-neath the tree of life,
And o'er its ho-ly beau-ty, Floats not a cloud of care,
There comes no wail of mourning, Nor sound of bit-ter strife.

Chorus.

Land of per-fect beau-ty, World so bright and fair;
When will an-gels call me, When shall I be there.

2.
There are the sweet voiced angels,
Around the great white throne,
Who bow in willing homage,
To him who rules above,
Death guards the mystic portals,
And gently one by one,
He leads in weary mortals,
Whose earthly work is done.
CHO.—Land of, &c.

3.
They stand before the Father,
The Lord of life and love ;
He smiles upon his children,
He welcomes them above,
And all in joyous singing,
And peace forever more,
There in that far off country,
Upon that golden shore.
CHO.—He leads &c.

GENTLY LEAD US.

Dr. J. B. Herbert.

1. Gently, Lord, O gently lead us, Thro' this lonely vale of tears;
2. In the hour of pain and anguish, In the hour when death draws near,

Thro' the changes thou'st decreed us, Till our last great change appears,
Suf-fer not our hearts to lan-guish, Suf-fer not our souls to fear,

When temptation's darts as-sail us, When in devious paths we stray,
And, when mortal life is end-ed, Bid us on thy bosom rest,

Let thy goodness never fail us, Lead us in thy perfect way.
Till, by an-gel-bands attend-ed, We a-wake among the blest.

64. AT THE DOOR.

Rev. Alfred Taylor. From "Sabbath Songs," by per. L. Marshall.

"Behold, I stand at the door, and knock."—Rev. iii. 20.

1. My Saviour stands waiting, and knocks at the door, Has knock'd, and is knocking a-gain; I hear His kind voice; I'll re-ject Him no more, Nor let Him stand pleading in vain, In in-fi-nite mer-cy He came from above To ransom, to cleanse me from sin; I'll yield to the door of my heart; 'Tis open'd in welcome to Thee; Come in, bless-ed

2. O Saviour, my Ransom, Redeemer, and Friend, The Life, and the Truth, and the Way, On Thy pre-cious mer-it a-lone I de-pend: Dwell in me, and keep me, I pray. Thy goodness hath open'd the

AT THE DOOR. Concluded.

voice of His mer-ci-ful love, And let my dear Saviour come in.
Saviour, and nev-er de-part; Come in, with Thy mercy, to me.

Chorus.

Saviour, come in; Cleanse me from sin: Jesus, my Saviour, come in, come in,

En-ter the door, Waiting no more, Saviour, dear Saviour, come in.

SINNER! COME.

J. H. T.

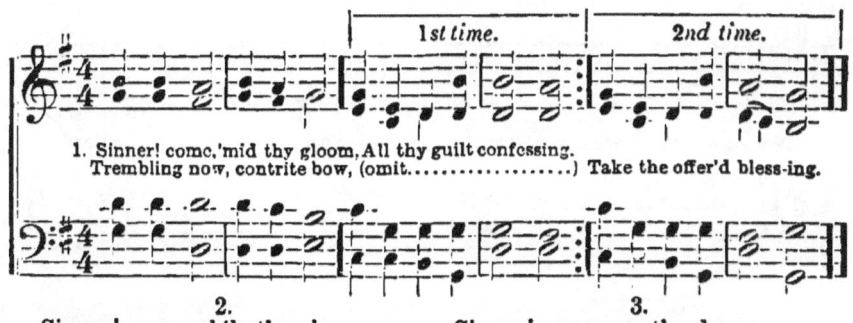

1st time.   2nd time.

1. Sinner! come, 'mid thy gloom, All thy guilt confessing.
Trembling now, contrite bow, (omit.................) Take the offer'd bless-ing.

2.
Sinner! come, while there's room—
While the feast is waiting;
While the Lord, by his word,
Kindly is inviting.

3.
Sinner! come, ere thy doom,
Shall be sealed forever;
Now return, grieve and mourn,
Flee to Christ, the Saviour.

3.
Nearer the bound where life
  Shall lay its burdens down;
Where I shall leave my ill-borne cross,
  And take my blood-bought crown.

4.
Saviour, perfect my trust,
  Confirm my feeble faith;
And teach me fearlessly to stand
  Upon the shore of death.

THE HARVEST IS PASSING.

J. H. TENNEY.

Earnestly.

1. Hark, sin-ner, while God from on high doth entreat thee, And
2. How oft of thy dan-ger and guilt hath he told thee, How

warnings with ac-cents of mer-cy doth blend, Give ear to his
oft still the mes-sage of mercy doth send, Haste, haste while he

voice, lest in judgment he meet thee, "The har-vest is passing, the
waits in his arms to en-fold thee, "The har-vest is passing, the

sum-mer will end, The harvest is passing, the summer will end."
sum-mer will end, The harvest is passing, the summer will end."

3. Despised, rejected, at length he may leave thee,
 What anguish and horror thy bosom may rend,
 Then haste thee, O sinner, while he will receive thee,
  "The harvest is passing, the summer will end."

4. The Saviour will call thee in judgment before him,
 O bow to his sceptre, and make him your friend,
 Now yield him thy heart and make haste to adore him,
  "Thy harvest is passing, thy summer will end."

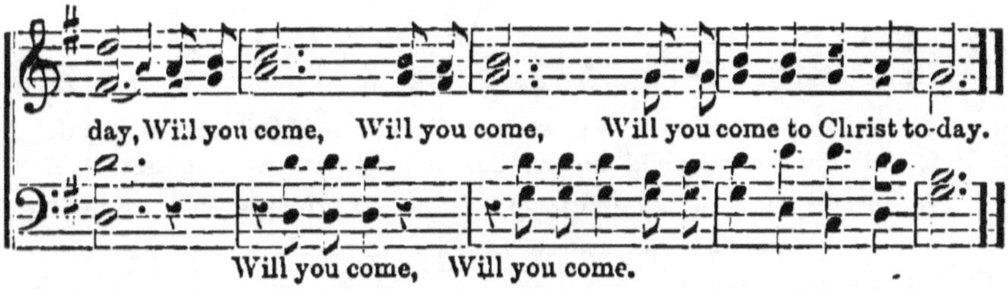

WILL YOU COME TO, &c. Concluded.

day, Will you come, Will you come, Will you come to Christ to-day.
Will you come, Will you come.

GLAD TIDINGS.

Mrs. E. C. Ellsworth.   From "Golden Sunbeams," by per.

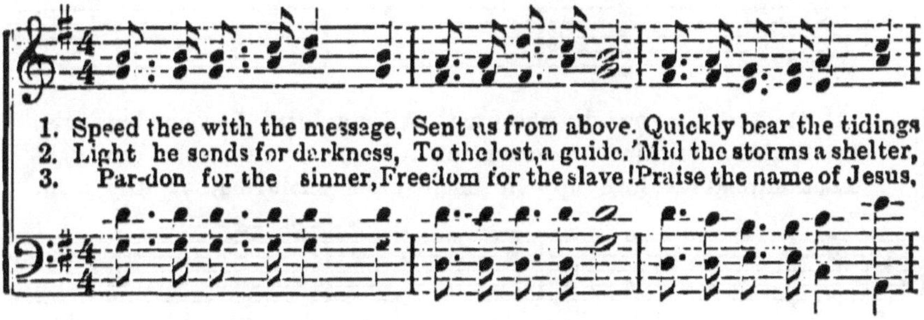

1. Speed thee with the message, Sent us from above. Quickly bear the tidings
2. Light he sends for darkness, To the lost, a guide. 'Mid the storms a shelter,
3. Par-don for the sinner, Freedom for the slave! Praise the name of Jesus,

Chorus.

Of a Saviour's love.   } Glad tid - ings, Glad tid - ings, Glad tidings of
Where the weary hide.   }
Sing his power to save.   }

Glad tidings of

joy, Go bear to the nations these tidings of joy: Glad tidings of joy.

joy;

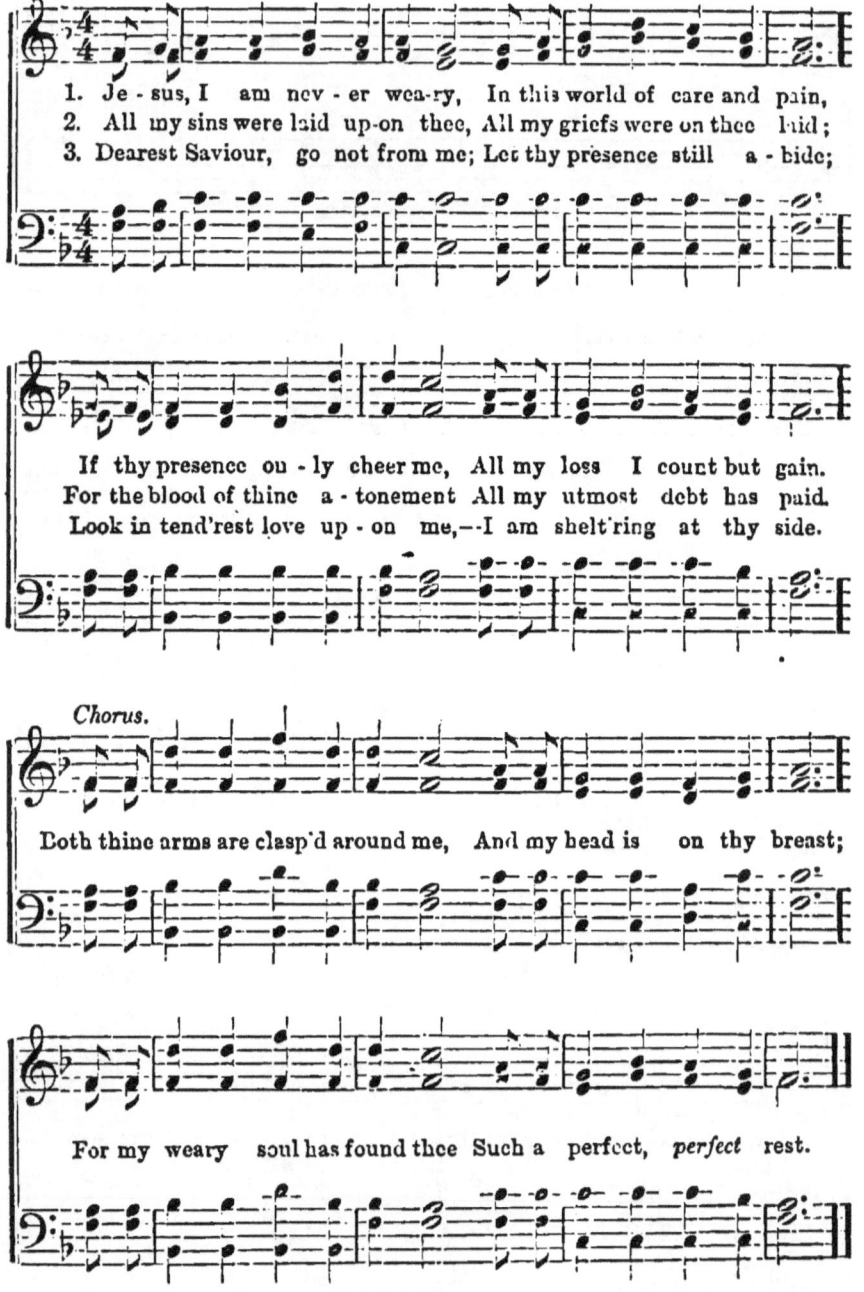

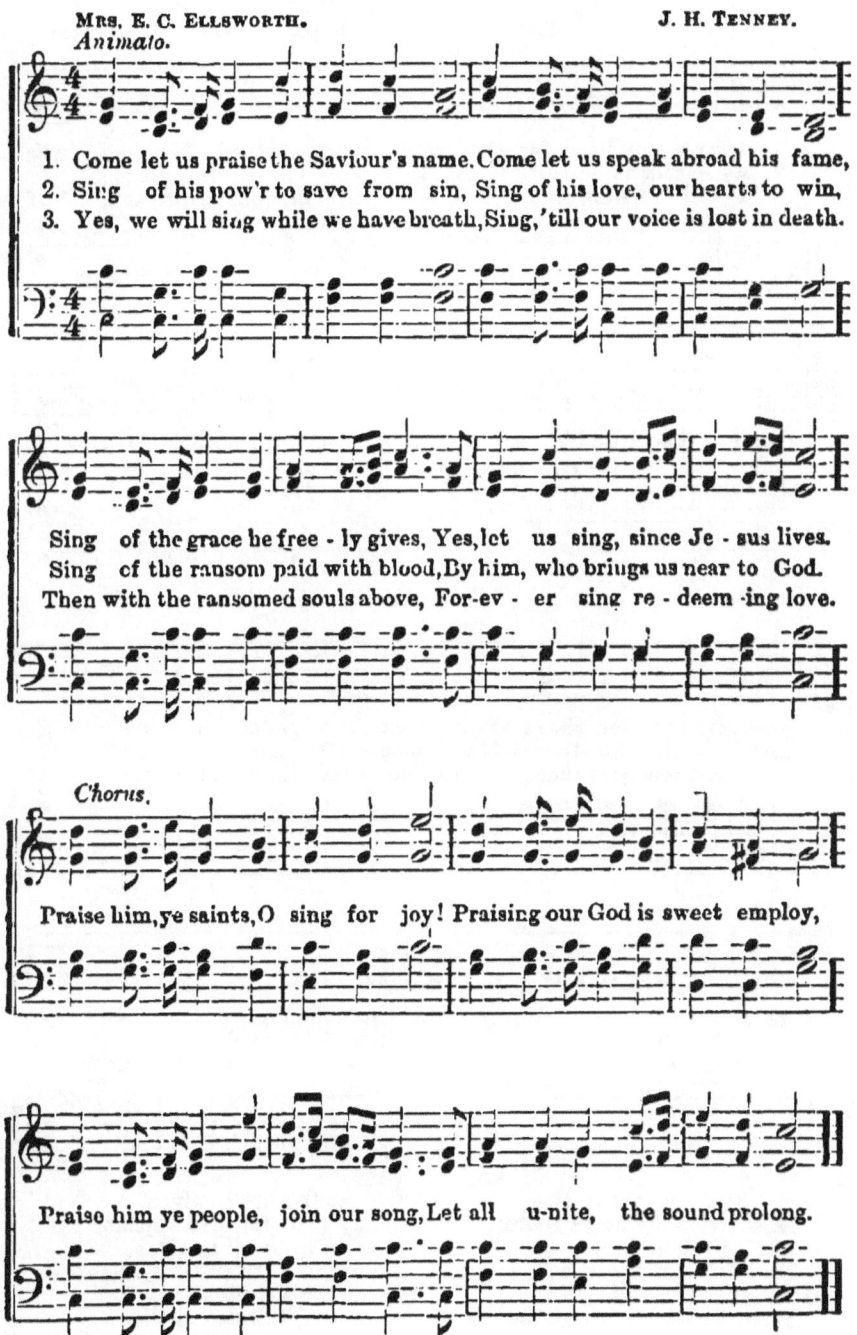

72   THIS I DID FOR THEE.

From "The Emerald," by per.   Dr. A. B. Everett.

1. I gave my life for thee, My precious blood I shed, That thou might'st ransom'd be, And quicken'd from the dead— I gave my life for thee; What hast thou giv'n for me? I gave my life for thee; What hast thou giv'n for me?

2. My Father's house of light, My rain-bow-circled throne I left for earth-ly night, For wand'rings sad and long— I left it all for thee; Hast thou left aught for me? I left it all for thee; Hast thou left aught for me?

3. I suf-fered much for thee, More than my tongue can tell, Of bit-terest a-go-ny, Thee to pre-serve from hell— I suf-fered much for thee; What do-est thou for me? I suffered much for thee; What do-est thou for me?

4. And I have brought to thee,
   Down from my home above,
 Salvation full and free,
   My spirit and my love;
 Great gifts I brought to thee;
 What hast thou brought to me?

5. Oh, let thy life be given,
   Thy years for me be spent,
 World-fetters all be riven,
   And joy with suffering blent—
 Give thou thyself to me,
 Gladly I'll welcome thee!

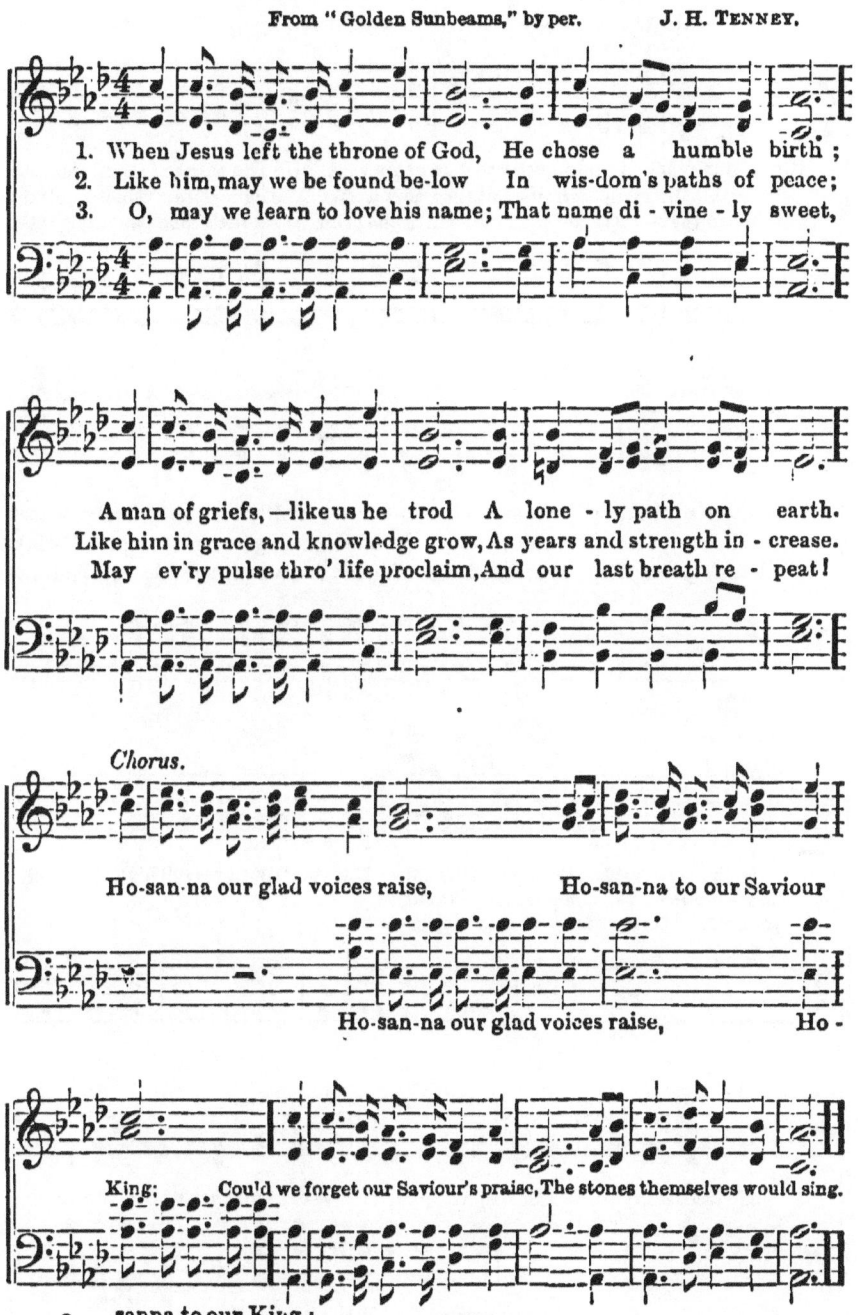

LET US PASS OVER, &c. Concluded.

rest under the shade, Rest un-der the shade of the trees."

THE WAY.

J. H. T.

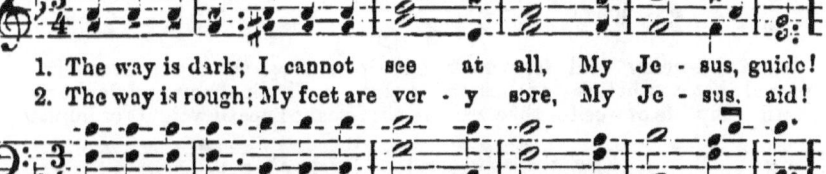

1. The way is dark; I cannot see at all, My Jesus, guide!
2. The way is rough; My feet are ver-y sore, My Jesus, aid!

Oh, let me feel the clasping of Thy hand Close by my side.
Oh, let me lean, while yet Thou lead-est on, Nor me up-braid.

3.
The way is long; I fear I yet may fall,
My Jesus, keep!
Oh, let my faith out-last the weary road,
No more to weep.

4.
The way, it ends! The radiant gate appears!
My Jesus fast!
My spirit hastes, and bounds with joy, to be
At home at last!

THE LOVE OF CHRIST. Concluded.

darkest, saddest hour, It can raise the weary soul from dark despair-ing.

4. Tempted, tried as thou hast been,
All thy sinning soul to win,
Hedged about with foes, and grieved with bitter scorning;
All for thee; sad soul be still!
Bow thee now unto my will,
Dark the night, but I will meet thee in the morning.

THE WATER OF LIFE.

FANNY CHURCH.   From "The Little Sower," by per.   J. H. TENNEY.

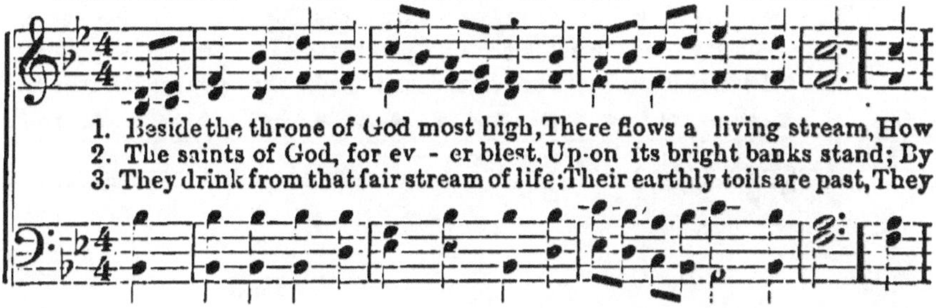

1. Beside the throne of God most high, There flows a living stream, How
2. The saints of God, for ev - er blest, Up-on its bright banks stand; By
3. They drink from that fair stream of life; Their earthly toils are past, They

Chorus.

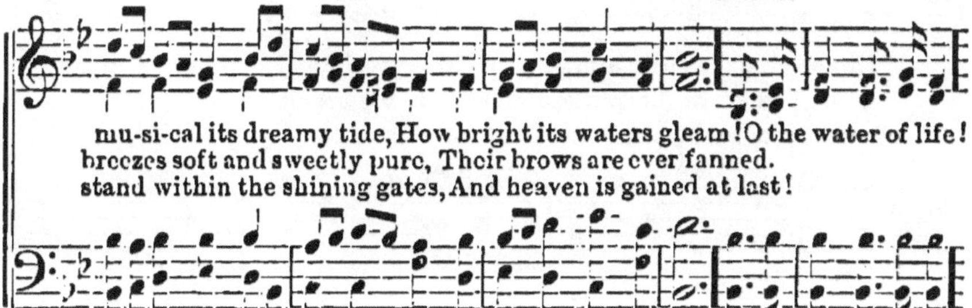

mu-si-cal its dreamy tide, How bright its waters gleam! O the water of life!
breezes soft and sweetly pure, Their brows are ever fanned.
stand within the shining gates, And heaven is gained at last!

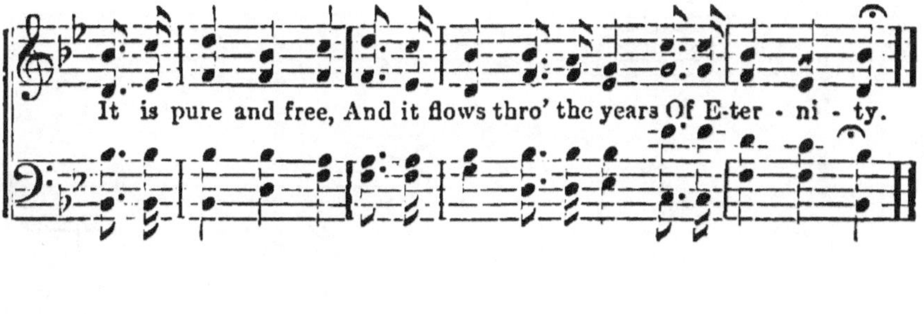

It is pure and free, And it flows thro' the years Of E-ter-ni-ty.

"I AM VERY HAPPY."

E. A. Hoffman. From the "Evergreen," by per. J. H. Tenney.

1. I am ver-y hap-py, Jesus loves me so; How my heart is warming With a heav'nly glow. Let me praise my Je-sus, Mag-ni-fy his name, Honor and exalt him, And his love proclaim. I am ver-y happy, Very, very hap-py, I am ver-y hap-py, Je-sus loves me so.

2. I am ver-y happy, Christ is all my song; Strains of joy I'm hymning Singing all day long. Christ is ver-y precious; I am tru-ly blest; I will try to keep him Reigning in my breast.

3. I am ver-y hap-py, Jesus loves me so; He will guard and keep me While I dwell below; And when life is end-ed, On yon golden shore Sweeter joys will greet me, Bliss for-ev-er more.

WHERE ARE THE NINE? 79

By permission. Words and Music by P. P. BLISS.
Read Luke xvii. 12 19.

3.
"Who is this Nazarene?" Pharisees say;
"Is he the Christ? tell us plainly, we pray."
Multitudes follow him seeking a sign,
Show them his mighty works—Where are the nine? CHO.

4.
Jesus on trial to-day we can see,
Thousands deridingly ask, "Who is he?"
How they're rejecting him, your Lord and mine!
Bring in the witnesses—Where are the nine? CHO.

ONWARD, CHRISTIAN, &c. Concluded. 81

COME TO JESUS.

2. He will save you, &c.
3. Oh, believe him.
4. He is able.
5. He is willing.
6. He'll receive you.
7. Call upon him.

8. He will hear you.
9. Look unto him.
10. He'll forgive you.
11. He will cleanse you.
12. Jesus loves you.
13. Only trust him.

NOTHING BUT LEAVES.

J. H. Tenney

3.
Nothing but leaves, sad memory weaves ;
  No vail to hide the past,
And as we trace our weary way,
Counting each lost and misspent day,
  Sadly we find at last—
  ‖: Nothing but leaves! :‖

4.
Ah! who shall thus the Master meet,
  Bearing but withered leaves?
Ah! who shall at the Saviour's feet,
Before the awful judgment-seat
  Lay down, for golden sheaves
  ‖: Nothing but leaves! :‖

THE BRIGHT FOREVER.

J. H. Tenney.

1. Shall we meet beyond the riv-er, Where the surges cease to roll;
2. Shall we meet in yon-der cit-y, Where the towers of crystal shine?
3. Shall we meet with Christ, our Saviour, When he comes to claim his own?

Where in all the bright for-ev-er, Sor-row ne'er shall press the soul?
Where the walls are all of jas-per, Built by workmanship di-vine?
Shall we know His blessed fa-vor, And behold Him on His throne?

Shall we meet in that blest har-bor, When our stormy voyage is o'er?
Shall we meet with many a lov'd one, That was torn from our embrace?
Far be-yond this world of sor-row, On fair Canaan's peaceful shore,

Shall we meet, and cast the an-chor By the fair ce-les-tial shore?
Shall we lis-ten to their voi-ces, And be-hold them face to face?
We shall meet, and with our Saviour, Dwell in love for-ev-er-more.

THE LAND OF BLISS. Concluded.

JESUS PAID IT ALL.

J. H. TENNEY.

2. When he from his lofty throne,
   Stoop'd down to do and die,
   Every thing was fully done,
   " 'Tis finish'd!" was his cry.
   CHO.

3. Clinging to the Saviour's cross,
   Look up by simple faith,
   Praise him for the pard'ning love
   That saves from endless death.
   CHO.

4. Bring a willing sacrifice—
   Thy soul to Jesus' feet;
   Stand in him, in him alone,
   All glorious and complete. CHO.

3. 'Tis a home of repose, where the sad and the weary,
Find rest from their labor, and nevermore roam;
Where prospects of happiness never grow dreary—
Come, go with the saints to their Paradise home.
Ye weary—ye weary.
Come go with the saints to their Paradise home.

4. There the bright morning stars with the angels are singing,
And praising Jehovah, who sits on his throne;
The portals of heaven with their anthems are ringing—
Come, go with the saints to their Paradise home.
Oh sinners! Oh sinners!
Come, go with the saints to their Paradise home.

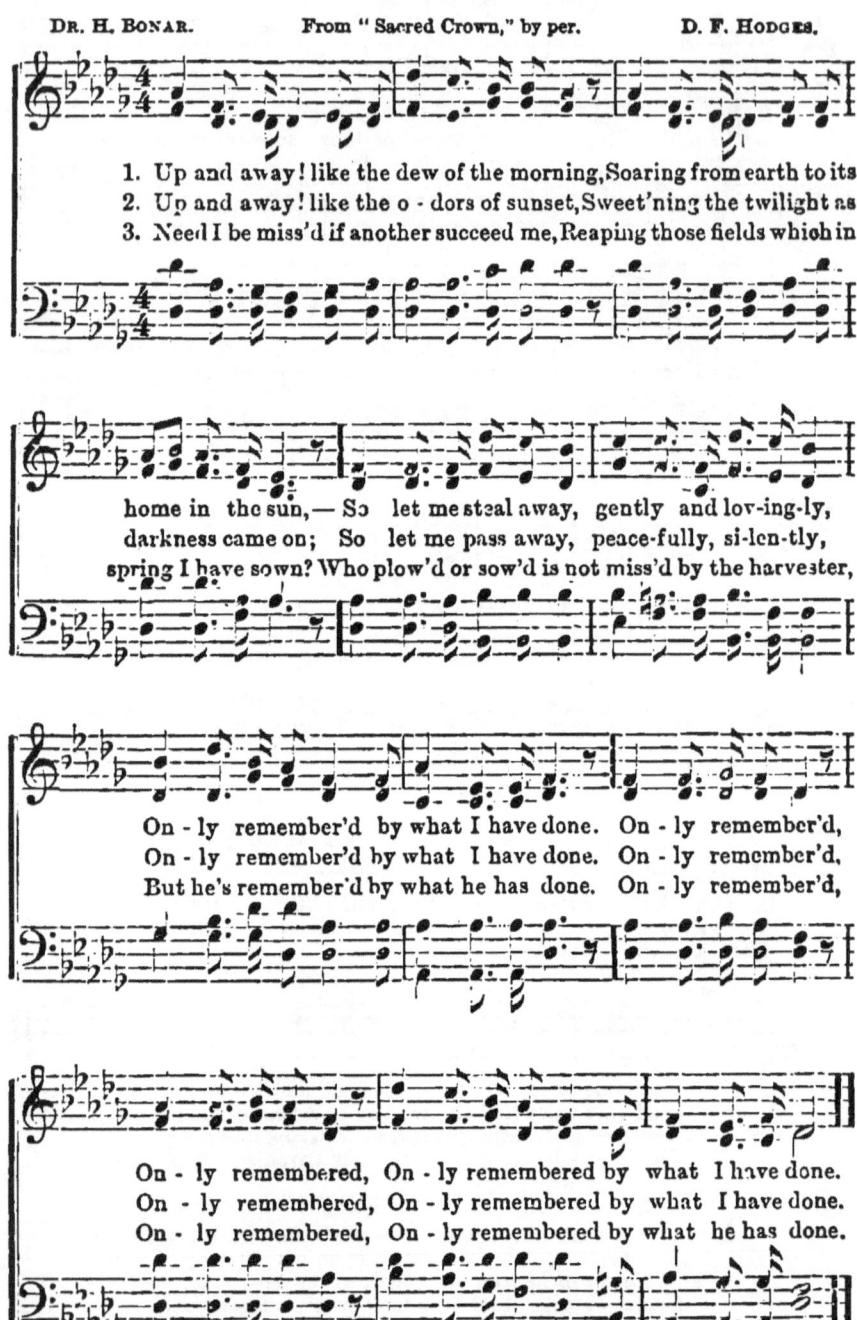

NEARING THE BETTER LAND. 91

W. A. SPATE. Arr. by J. H. TENNEY.

1. Careworn trav'ler on life's o - cean, Bound for yonder golden strand,
2. Tho' the sky be dark and gloom - y, And the wild storms loudly roar,
3. Trust in God and be not fear - ful, He will lend a helping hand;

Look beyond the waves' commo - tion, Thou art nearing that blest land.
Look with hopeful heart beyond them, Thou art nearing yon blest shore.
Let thy heart be light and cheer-ful, Thou art near the better land.

Refrain.

Nearing, nearing, nearing, nearing, Thou art nearing that blest land.

Tune, "CHRIST THE REFUGE," on page 90.

4.
We are the wanderers
    Rocked on the foam,
Sad and sick, weak and worn,
    Far from our home;
Sighing in loneliness,
    Seeking in vain
Rest from our weariness,
    Ease from our pain.

5.
Speak to our troubled hearts,
    Saviour divine,
Say to the tired and weak,
    "Peace thou art mine;"
Glad to this sheltering Rock,
    Dear Lord, we flee,
None ever sought in vain
    Refuge in Thee.

MY SWEET HOME, &c. Concluded.

SECURITY. S. M.

L. AUSTIN. From "Morning Star," by per. D. F. HODGES.

2.
Whether we sleep or wake,
  To thee we both resign ;
By night we see, as well as day,
  If thy light on us shine.

3.
O thou, our soul's chief hope!
  We to thy mercy fly ;
Where'er we are, thou canst protect;
  Whate'er we need supply.

94. BE NOT DISCOURAGED.

R. G. STAPLES. From "Golden Sheaf," by per. J. H. TENNEY.

1. Be not discouraged, burden'd one, Tho' tears of anguish fill thine eyes;
2. Re-mem-ber sad Gethsemane, Thou who wouldst mourn thy sad estate,
3. Be not discouraged, stricken one; But weep, if weeping will relieve

Though earthly prospects seem undone, And even hope within thee dies.
And, look-ing up to Cal-va-ry, Repent thee, ere it is too late.
Thy breaking heart—for God's dear Son Oft wept, and why should we not grieve?

Does not the Man of Sorrows live? The Man who wept and shed his blood,
For Je-sus wept, and may not we Find con-so-la-tion in our tears—
Grieve that our sins oppress us sore, Weep that we live so far from God,

That to the wea-ry he might give Redemption thro' its crimson flood.
Through sad a-flic-tion ev-er see The hand that chastens, likewise cheers.
Yes, weep, and but rejoice the more, If chastened often by his rod.

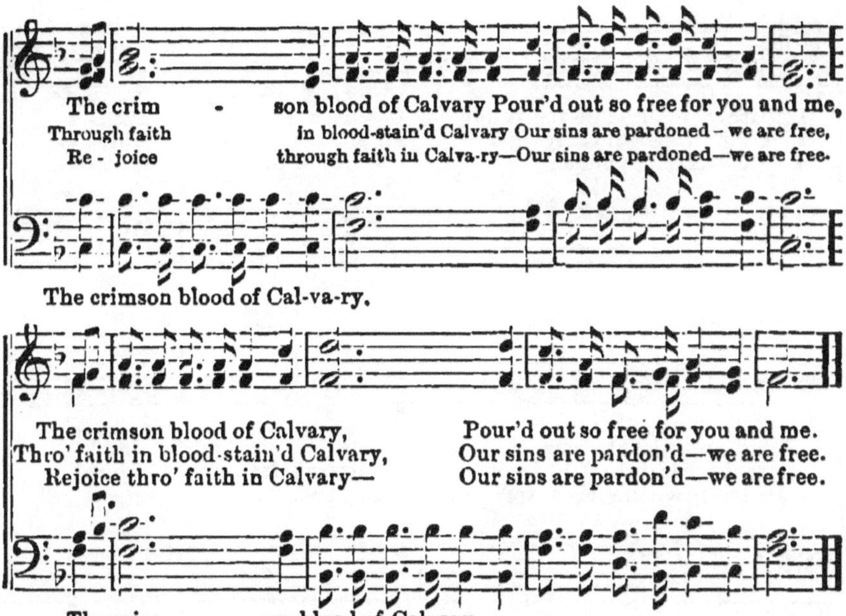

BE NOT DISCOURAGED. Concluded.

The crim - son blood of Calvary Pour'd out so free for you and me,
Through faith in blood-stain'd Calvary Our sins are pardoned – we are free,
Re - joice through faith in Calva-ry—Our sins are pardoned—we are free.

The crimson blood of Cal-va-ry.

The crimson blood of Calvary,   Pour'd out so free for you and me.
Thro' faith in blood-stain'd Calvary,   Our sins are pardon'd—we are free.
Rejoice thro' faith in Calvary—   Our sins are pardon'd—we are free.

The crim - son blood of Calvary.

JUST AS I AM.

O. W. PILLSBURY.

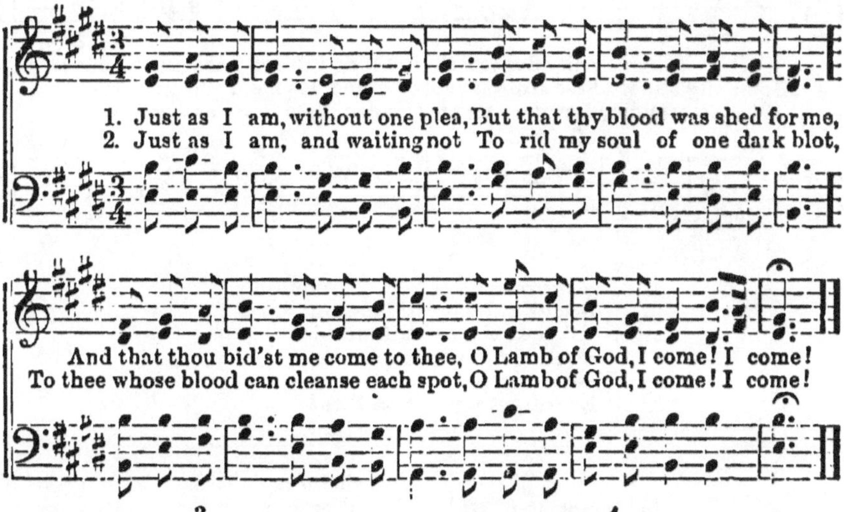

1. Just as I am, without one plea, But that thy blood was shed for me,
2. Just as I am, and waiting not To rid my soul of one dark blot,

And that thou bid'st me come to thee, O Lamb of God, I come! I come!
To thee whose blood can cleanse each spot, O Lamb of God, I come! I come!

3.
Just as I am—thou wilt receive,
Wilt welcome, pardon, cleanse, relieve;
Because thy promise I believe,
O Lamb of God, I come!

4.
Just as I am—thy love unknown
Hath broken every barrier down;
Now, to be thine, yes, thine alone,
O Lamb of God, I come!

96. THE NEW JERUSALEM.

DR. BONAR. J. R. MURRAY.

1. Bathed in un-fail-ing sun-light, It-self a sun-born gem,....
2. Calm in her queenly glo-ry, She sits all joy and light,....
3. Shad-ing her gold-en pave-ment, The tree of life is seen,....

Fair gleams the glorious cit-y, The new Je-ru-sa-lem!
Pure in her bri-dal beau-ty, Her raiment fes-tal white!
Its fruit-rich branches wav-ing, Ce-les-tial ev-er-green.

Cit-y fairest, Splendor rarest, Let me, let me gaze on thee!
Home of gladness, Free from sadness, Let me, let me dwell in thee!
Tree of wonder, Let me under, Under thee for-ev-er rest!

4.
Fresh from the throne of Godhead,
 Bright in its crystal gleam,
Bursts out the living fountain,
 Swells on the living stream.
Blessed river, Let me ever,
 Ever feast my eye on thee!

5.
Stream of true life and gladness,
 Spring of all health and peace;
No harps by thee hang silent,
 Nor happy voices cease.
Tranquil river, Let me ever,
 Ever sit and sing by thee!

HE CARETH FOR THEE.

J. R. MURRAY.

1. Voy-a-ger o'er life's rough tide, Cast thy haunting fears a-side,
2. Mourner sit-ting dumb with pain, Do not murmur or complain;
3. Toil-er in life's dust-y ways, Dragging thro' the weary days,

He who walked in Gal-i-lee Walks as sure-ly by thy
He by sor-rows sore-ly tried Shall be crowned with joy a-
When the vail is rent in twain, Thou shalt see with sweet a-

side, Tho' thou canst not hear or see.
gain, 'Mong the hosts of pu-ri-fied. } He car-eth for thee.
maze, Not a stripe was borne in vain.

Tune, "COWPER," page 114.

1.
There is a safe and secret place
 Beneath the wings divine,
Reserved for all the heirs of grace:
 Oh, be that refuge mine!

2.
The least and feeblest there may hide,
 Uninjured and unawed ;
While thousands fall on every side,
 He rests secure in God.

3.
He feeds in pastures large and fair,
 Of love and truth divine ;
O child of God, O glory's heir!
 How rich a lot is thine!

4.
A hand almighty to defend,
 An ear for every call,
An honored life, a peaceful end,
 And heaven to crown it all!

GERALD. 6s & 4s.

From the "Morning Star," by per.   J. H. TENNEY

1. Nearer, my God, to thee, Nearer to thee! E'en tho' it be a cross That raiseth me, Still all my song shall be, Nearer, my God, to thee, Nearer to Thee! Nearer to thee.

2.
Though like a wanderer,
  The sun gone down,
Darkness comes over me,
  My rest a stone;
Yet in my dreams I'd be
Nearer, my God, to thee,
  Nearer to thee!

3.
There let the way appear
  Steps unto heaven;
All that thou sendest me
  In mercy given;
Angels to beckon me
Nearer, my God, to thee,
  Nearer to thee!

4.
Then with my waking thoughts,
  Bright with thy praise,
Out of my stony griefs,
  Bethel I'll raise;
So by my woes to be
Nearer, my God, to thee,
  Nearer to thee.

5.
Or, if on joyful wing,
  Cleaving the sky,
Sun, moon, and stars forgot,
  Upward I fly,
Still all my song shall be,
  Nearer, my God, to thee,
    Nearer to thee.

3.
Up to that world of light,
Take us, dear Saviour!
May we all there unite,
Happy forever!
Where kindred spirits dwell,
There may our music swell,
And time our joys dispel
Never, no, never!

4.
Soon shall we meet again,
Meet ne'er to sever;
Soon will peace wreathe her chain
Round us forever;
Our hearts will then repose,
Secure from worldly woes:
Our songs of praise shall close
Never, no, never!

HAMBURG. L. M. Dr. L. Mason. 101

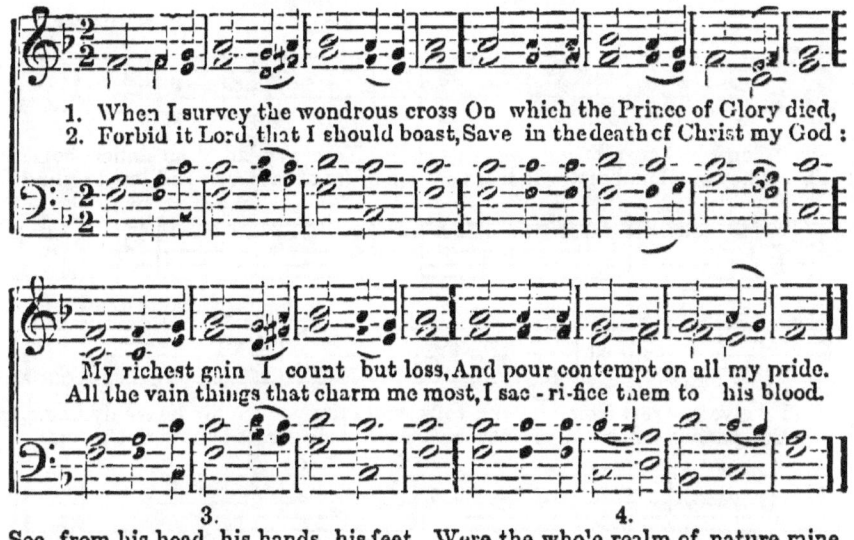

1. When I survey the wondrous cross On which the Prince of Glory died,
2. Forbid it Lord, that I should boast, Save in the death of Christ my God:
My richest gain I count but loss, And pour contempt on all my pride.
All the vain things that charm me most, I sac-ri-fice them to his blood.

3.
See, from his head, his hands, his feet,
Sorrow and love flow mingled down!
Did e'er such love and sorrow meet,
Or thorns compose so rich a crown?

4.
Were the whole realm of nature mine,
That were an off'ring far too small:
Love so amazing, so divine,
Demands my soul, my life, my all!

DUKE STREET. L. M. J. Hatton.

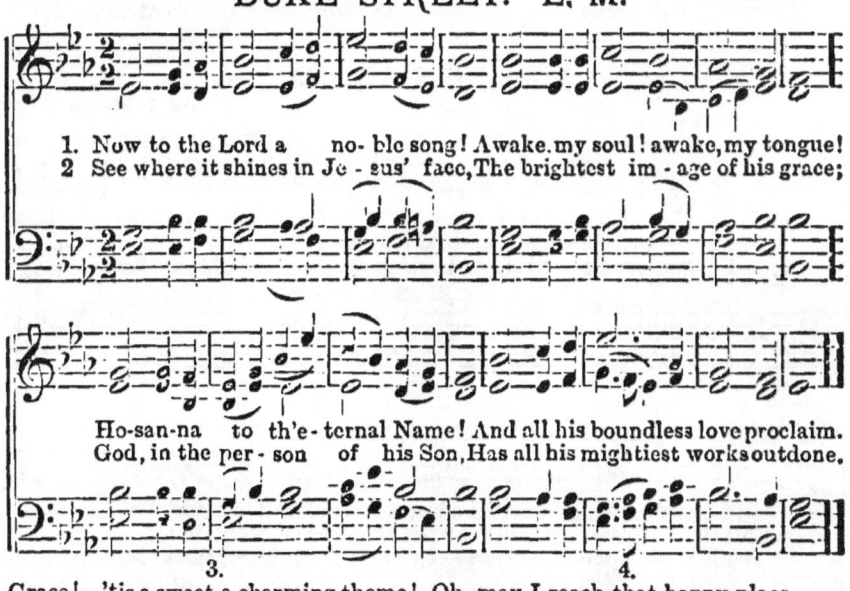

1. Now to the Lord a no-ble song! Awake, my soul! awake, my tongue!
2. See where it shines in Je-sus' face, The brightest im-age of his grace;
Ho-san-na to th'e-ternal Name! And all his boundless love proclaim.
God, in the per-son of his Son, Has all his mightiest works outdone.

3.
Grace!—'tis a sweet, a charming theme!
My thoughts rejoice at Jesus' name;
Ye angels, dwell upon the sound;
Ye heavens, reflect it to the ground!

4.
Oh, may I reach that happy place
Where he unveils his lovely face,
Where all his beauties you behold,
And sing his name to harps of gold.

FEDERAL STREET. L. M.

H. K. OLIVER.

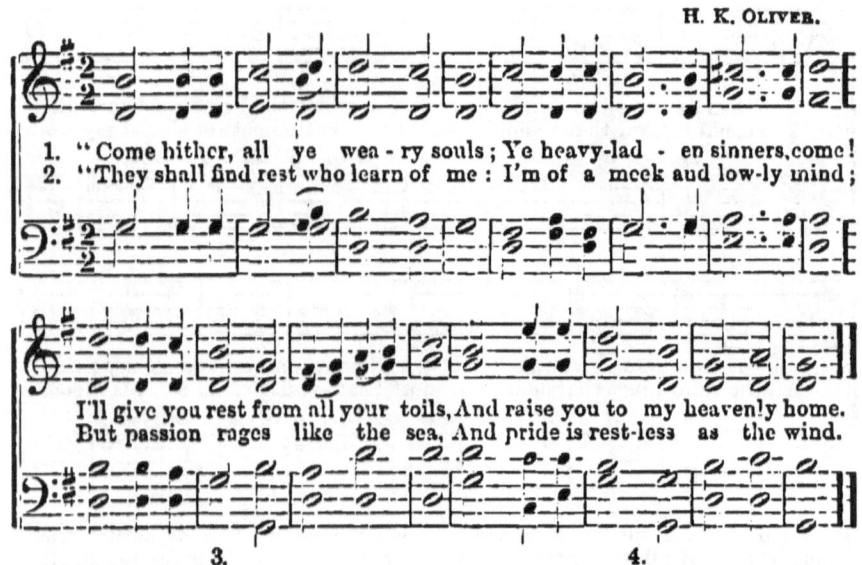

1. "Come hither, all ye wea-ry souls; Ye heavy-lad-en sinners, come!
2. "They shall find rest who learn of me: I'm of a meek and low-ly mind;

I'll give you rest from all your toils, And raise you to my heavenly home.
But passion rages like the sea, And pride is rest-less as the wind.

3.
"Blest is the man whose shoulders take
  My yoke, and bear it with delight:
My yoke is easy to his neck, [light."
  My grace shall make the burden

4.
Jesus, we come at thy command;
  With faith, and hope, and humble
Resign our spirits to thy hand, [zeal,
  To mold and guide us at thy will.

HEBRON. L. M.

DR. L. MASON.

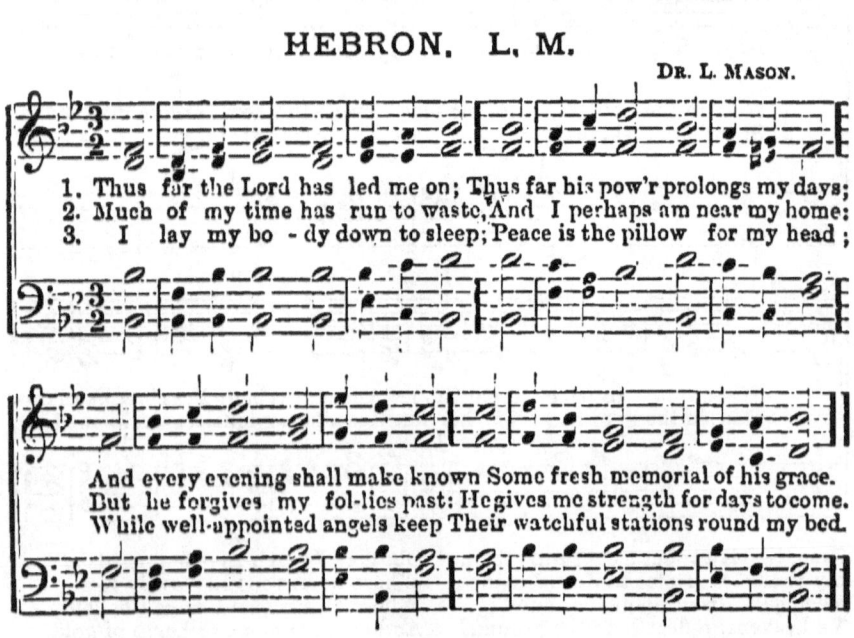

1. Thus far the Lord has led me on; Thus far his pow'r prolongs my days;
2. Much of my time has run to waste, And I perhaps am near my home:
3. I lay my bo-dy down to sleep; Peace is the pillow for my head;

And every evening shall make known Some fresh memorial of his grace.
But he forgives my fol-lies past: He gives me strength for days to come.
While well-appointed angels keep Their watchful stations round my bed.

SESSIONS. L. M.

L. O. EMERSON.

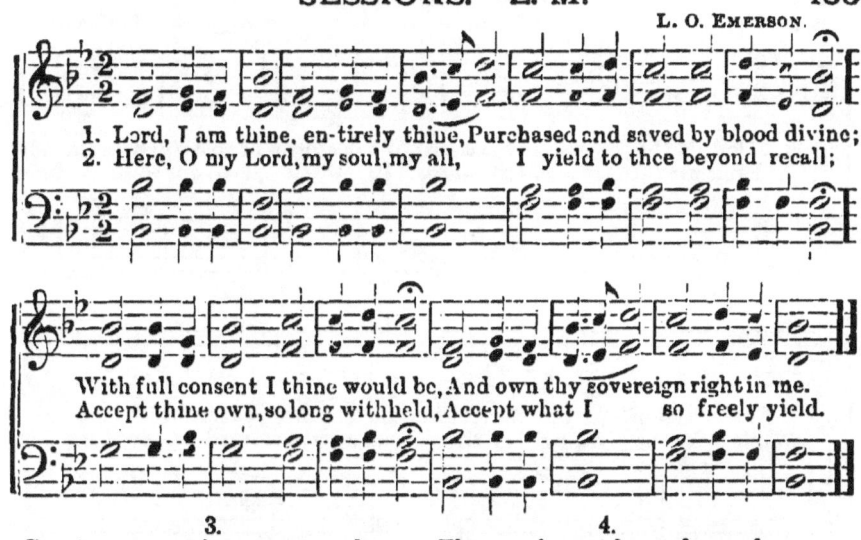

1. Lord, I am thine, entirely thine, Purchased and saved by blood divine;
With full consent I thine would be, And own thy sovereign right in me.
2. Here, O my Lord, my soul, my all, I yield to thee beyond recall;
Accept thine own, so long withheld, Accept what I so freely yield.

3.
Grant one poor sinner more a place
Among the children of thy grace;
A wretched sinner lost to God,
But ransomed by Immanuel's blood.

4.
The vow is past beyond repeal;
Now will I set the solemn seal:
Thine would I live, thine would I die,
Be thine through all eternity.

ROCKINGHAM. L. M.

DR. L. MASON.

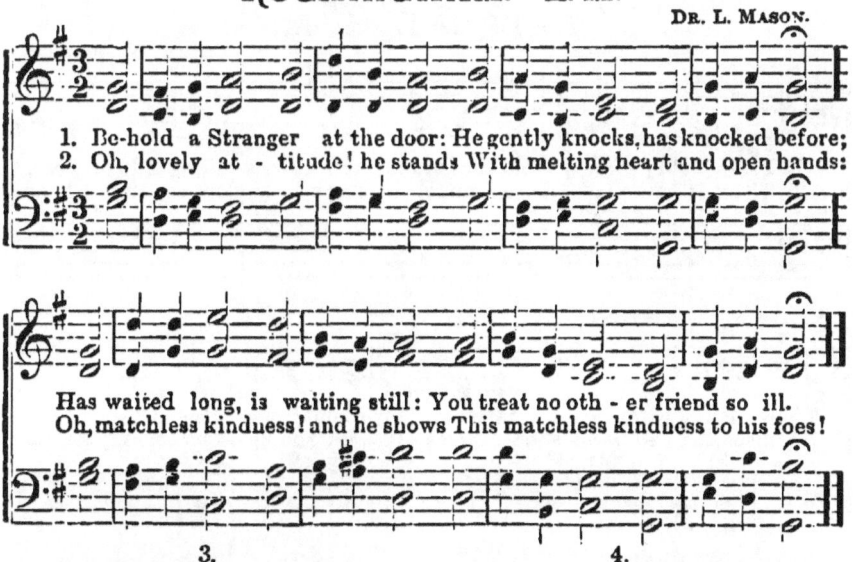

1. Behold a Stranger at the door: He gently knocks, has knocked before;
Has waited long, is waiting still: You treat no other friend so ill.
2. Oh, lovely attitude! he stands With melting heart and open hands:
Oh, matchless kindness! and he shows This matchless kindness to his foes!

3.
Rise, touched with gratitude divine,
Turn out his enemy and thine;
Turn out thy soul-enslaving sin,
And let the heavenly Stranger in.

4.
Oh, welcome him, the Prince of Peace!
Now may his gentle reign increase!
Throw wide the door, each willing mind;
And be his empire all mankind.

WARD. L. M.

Arr. by Dr. L. Mason.

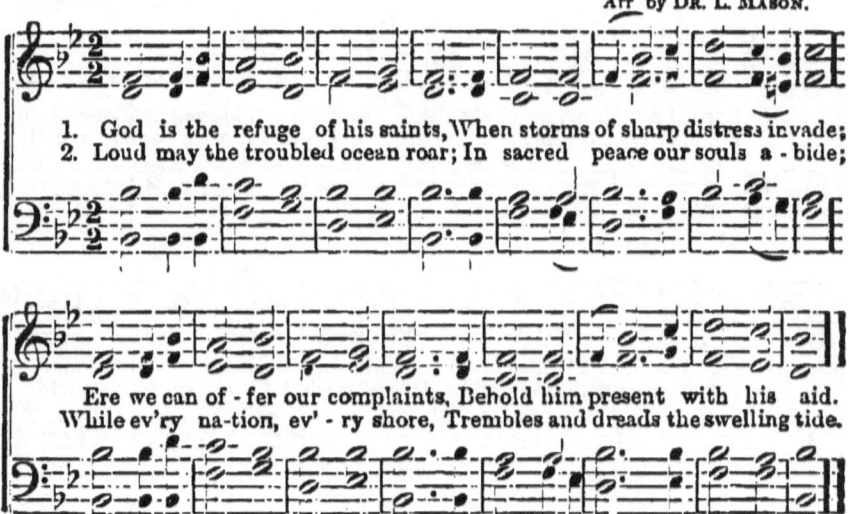

1. God is the refuge of his saints, When storms of sharp distress invade;
Ere we can offer our complaints, Behold him present with his aid.
2. Loud may the troubled ocean roar; In sacred peace our souls abide;
While ev'ry nation, ev'ry shore, Trembles and dreads the swelling tide.

3. There is a stream, whose gentle flow
Supplies the city of our God,
Life, love and joy, still gliding thro',
And watering our divine abode.

4. That sacred stream, thine holy word,
Our grief allays, our fear controls;
Sweet peace thy promises afford,
And give new strength to fainting [souls.

RETREAT. L. M.

Dr. T. Hastings.

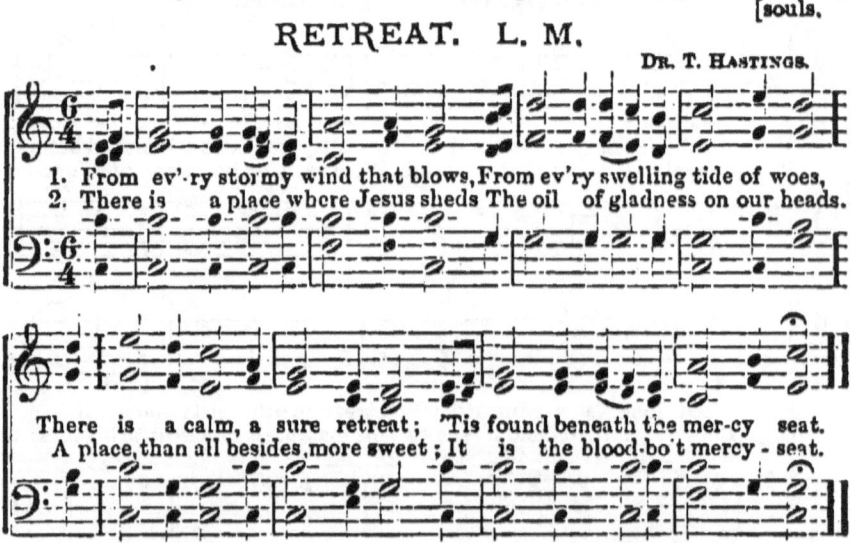

1. From ev'ry stormy wind that blows, From ev'ry swelling tide of woes,
There is a calm, a sure retreat; 'Tis found beneath the mercy seat.
2. There is a place where Jesus sheds The oil of gladness on our heads.
A place, than all besides, more sweet; It is the blood-bo't mercy-seat.

3. There is a scene where spirits blend,
Where friend holds fellowship with [friend;
Tho' sunder'd far, by faith they meet
Around one common mercy-seat!

4. Oh! let my hand forget her skill,
My tongue be silent, cold, and still,
This throbbing heart forget to beat,
If I forget the mercy-seat.

WELLS. L. M.

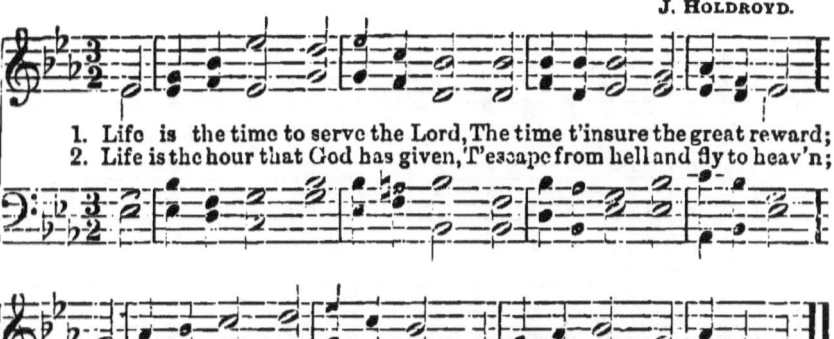

1. Life is the time to serve the Lord, The time t'insure the great reward;
2. Life is the hour that God has given, T'escape from hell and fly to heav'n;

And while the lamp holds out to burn, The vilest sin-ner may return.
The day of grace,—and mortals may Secure the blessings of the day.

3.
Then what my thoughts design to do,
My hands, with all your might pursue,
Since no device, nor work is found,
Nor faith, nor hope, beneath the ground.

4.
There are no acts of pardon passed
In the cold ground to which we haste;
But darkness, death, and long despair
Reign in eternal silence there.

WINDHAM. L. M.

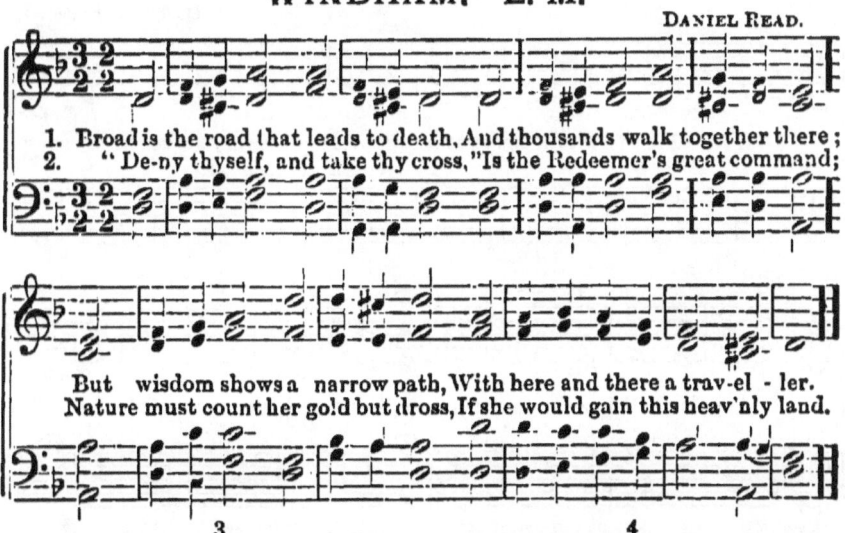

1. Broad is the road that leads to death, And thousands walk together there;
2. "De-ny thyself, and take thy cross," Is the Redeemer's great command;

But wisdom shows a narrow path, With here and there a trav-el-ler.
Nature must count her gold but dross, If she would gain this heav'nly land.

3
The fearful soul that tires and faints,
And walks the ways of God no more,
Is but esteemed almost a saint,
And makes his own destruction sure.

4
Lord! let not all my hopes be vain;
Create my heart entirely new:
Which hypocrites could ne'er attain;
Which false apostates never knew.

ROSCOE. L. M.

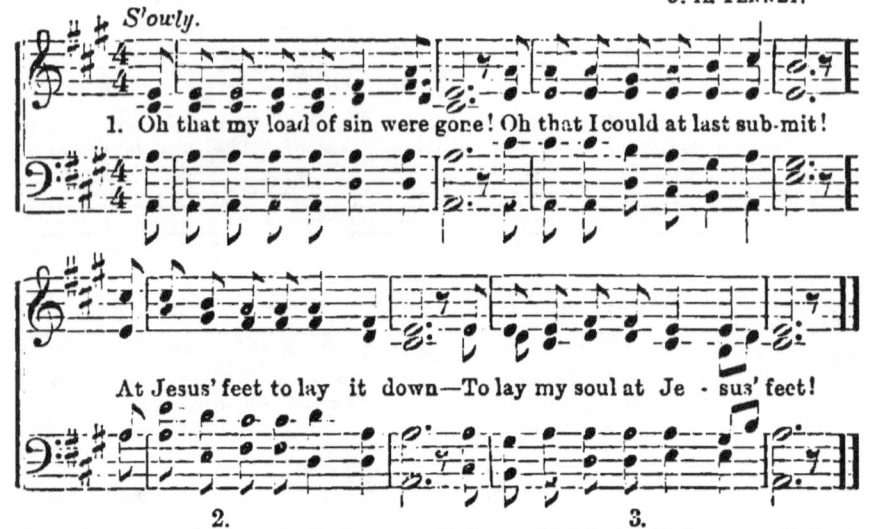

J. H. Tenney.

1. Oh that my load of sin were gone! Oh that I could at last sub-mit! At Jesus' feet to lay it down—To lay my soul at Je-sus' feet!

2.
Rest for my soul I long to find:
Saviour of all, if mine thou art,
Give me thy meek and lowly mind,
And stamp thy image on my heart.

3.
Fain would I learn of thee, my God;
Thy light and easy burden prove,—
The cross all stained with hallowed
The labor of thy dying love. [blood,

TOURJEE. L. M.

J. H. Tenney, 1867.

1. With all my pow'rs of heart and tongue, I'll praise my Maker in my song; Angels shall hear the notes I raise, Approve the song, and join the praise.

2.
Amid a thousand snares, I stand
Upheld and guarded by thy hand;
Thy words my fainting soul revive,
And keep my dying faith alive.

3.
I'll sing thy truth and mercy, Lord,
I'll sing the wonders of thy word;
Not all thy works and names below
So much thy power and glory show.

SCARBOROUGH. C. M.

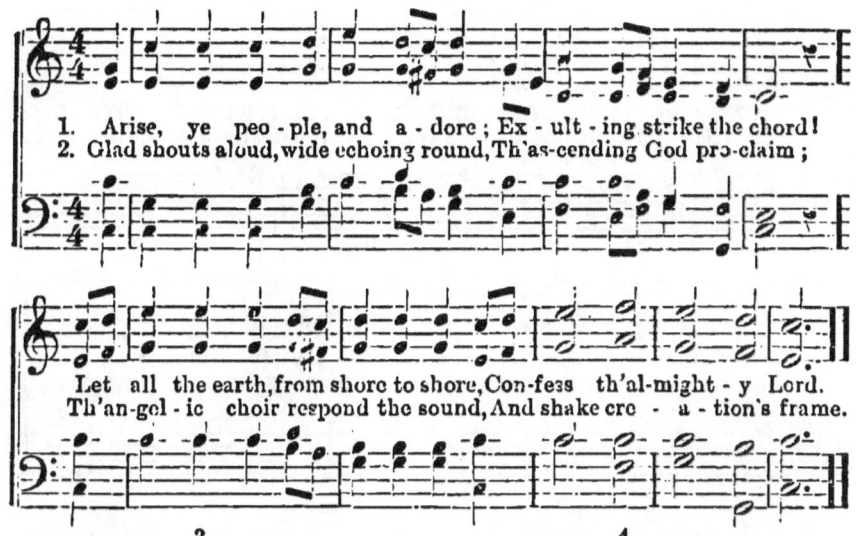

1. Arise, ye peo-ple, and a-dore; Ex-ult-ing strike the chord!
2. Glad shouts aloud, wide echoing round, Th'as-cending God proclaim;

Let all the earth, from shore to shore, Con-fess th'al-might-y Lord.
Th'an-gel-ic choir respond the sound, And shake cre-a-tion's frame.

3.
They sing of death and hell o'erthrown
In that triumphant hour;
And God exalts his conqu'ring Son
To his right hand of power.

4.
Oh, shout, ye people, and adore;
Exulting strike the chord!
Let all the earth, from shore to shore,
Confess th' almighty Lord!

DUNDEE. C. M.

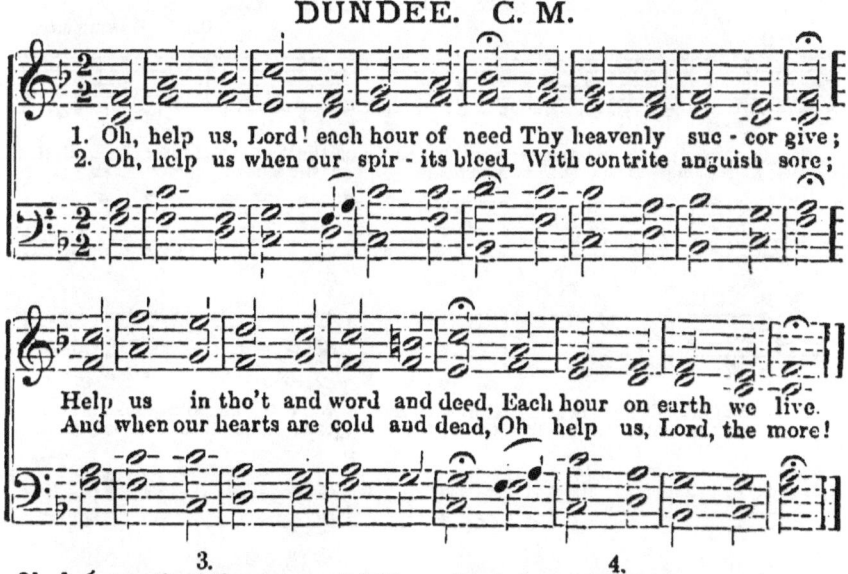

1. Oh, help us, Lord! each hour of need Thy heavenly suc-cor give;
2. Oh, help us when our spir-its bleed, With contrite anguish sore;

Help us in tho't and word and deed, Each hour on earth we live.
And when our hearts are cold and dead, Oh help us, Lord, the more!

3.
Oh, help us, thro' the prayer of faith,
More firmly to believe!
For still the more the servant hath,
The more shall he receive.

4.
Oh, help us, Jesus! from on high;
We know no help but thee;
Oh, help us so to live and die,
As thine in heaven to be!

MARLOW. C. M.

English Melody.

1. Sing, ye re-deem-ed of the Lord, Your great De-liv'-rer sing;
2. His hand divine shall lead you on Through all the bliss-ful road,

Pilgrims for Zi-on's cit-y bound, Be joy-ful in your King.
Till to the sa-cred mount you rise, And see your smil-ing God.

3.
There garlands of immortal joy
Shall bloom on every head;
While sorrow, sighing, and distress,
Like shadows, all are fled.

4.
March on in your Redeemer's strength;
Pursue his footsteps still;
And let the prospect cheer your eye,
While lab'ring up the hill

ORTONVILLE. C. M.

Dr. T. Hastings.

1. Ma-jes-tic sweetness sits enthroned Up-on the Saviour's brow; His head with
2. No mor-tal can with him compare, A-mong the sons of men: Fair-er is

radiant glories crowned, His lips with grace o'erflow. His lips with grace o'erflow.
he than all the fair That fill the heavenly train, That fill the heavenly train.

3.
To him I owe my life and breath,
And all the joys I have;
He makes me triumph over death,
He saves me from the grave.

4.
Since from his bounty I receive
Such proofs of love divine,
Had I a thousand hearts to give,
Lord! they should all be thine.

CORONATION. C. M.

OLIVER HOLDEN.

1. All hail, the power of Jesus' name! Let angels prostrate fall:
Bring forth the roy-al di-a-dem, And crown him Lord of all!
Bring forth the royal di-a-dem, And crown him Lord.... of all!

2. Crown him, ye martyrs of our God, Who from his al-tar call;
Extol the stem of Jes-se's rod, And crown him Lord of all!
Ex-tol the stem of Jes-se's rod, And crown him Lord.... of all!

3.
Ye chosen seed of Israel's race,
A remnant weak and small,
Hail him who saves you by his grace,
And crown him Lord of all!

4.
Ye Gentile sinners, ne'er forget
The wormwood and the gall;
Go, spread your trophies at his feet,
And crown him Lord of all!

"HOSANNA TO THE SON OF DAVID!"

1.
Hosanna! be our cheerful song
To Christ our Saviour King;
His praise, to whom we all belong,
Let all unite to sing.

2.
Hosanna! here in joyful bands,
Let old and young proclaim;
And hail, with voices, hearts, and hands,
The Son of David's name.

3.
Hosanna! sound from hill to hill,
And spread from plain to plain;
While louder, sweeter, clearer still,
Woods echo to the strain.

4.
Hosanna! on the wings of light,
O'er earth and ocean fly,
Till morn to eve, and noon to night,
And heaven to earth reply.

DEDHAM. C. M.

Wm. Gardiner.

1. Sweet was the time when first I felt The Saviour's pardoning blood
2. In pray'r, my soul drew near the Lord, And saw his glo-ry shine;

Applied to cleanse my soul from guilt, And bring me home to God.
And when I read his ho-ly word, I called each promise mine.

3.
Now, when the evening shade prevails,
My soul in darkness mourns;
And when the morn the light reveals,
No light to me returns.

4.
Rise, Saviour! help me to prevail,
And make my soul thy care;
I know thy mercy cannot fail,
Let me that mercy share.

PETERBORO'. C. M.

Ralph Harrison.

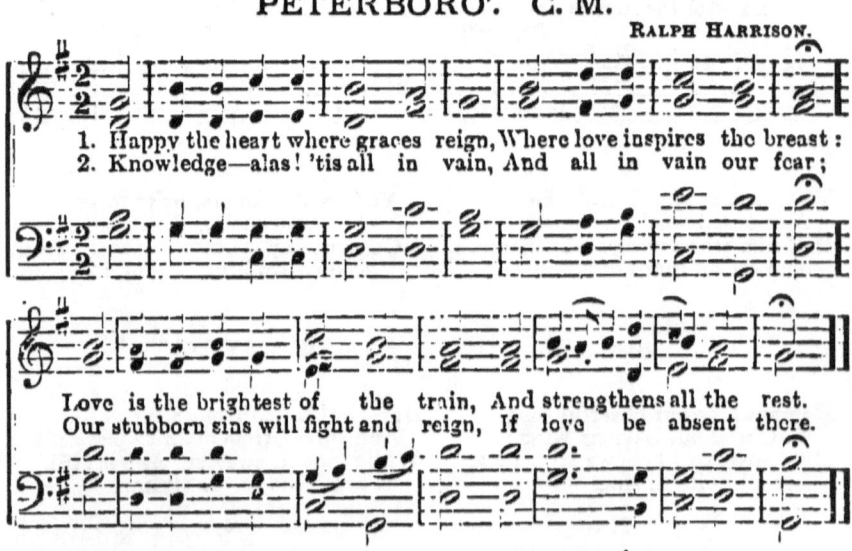

1. Happy the heart where graces reign, Where love inspires the breast:
2. Knowledge—alas! 'tis all in vain, And all in vain our fear;

Love is the brightest of the train, And strengthens all the rest.
Our stubborn sins will fight and reign, If love be absent there.

3.
This is the grace that lives and sings,
When faith and hope shall cease;
'Tis this shall strike our joyful strings,
In realms of endless peace.

4.
Before we quite forsake our clay,
Or leave this dark abode,
The wings of love bear us away,
To see our smiling God.

MEAR. C.M.

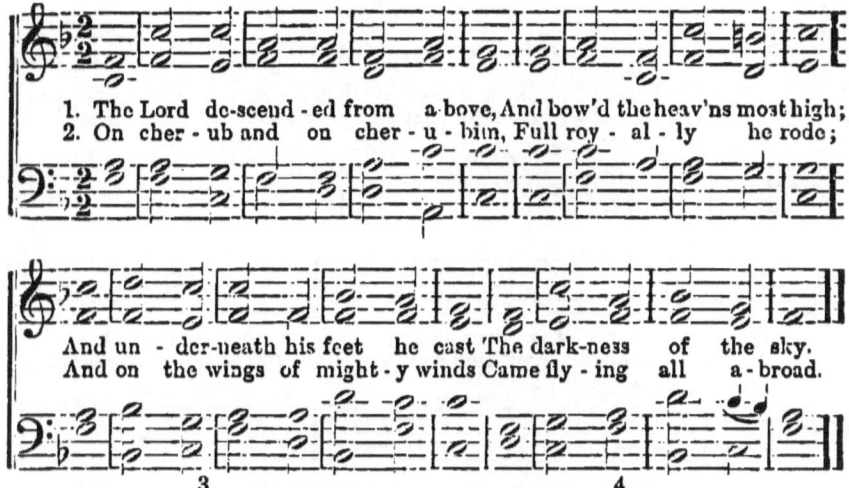

1. The Lord de-scend-ed from a-bove, And bow'd the heav'ns most high;
2. On cher-ub and on cher-u-bim, Full roy-al-ly he rode;

And un-der-neath his feet he cast The dark-ness of the sky.
And on the wings of might-y winds Came fly-ing all a-broad.

3.
The Lord will give his people strength,
Whereby they shall increase;
And he will bless his chosen flock
With everlasting peace.

4.
Give glory to his awful name,
And honor him alone;
Give worship to his majesty
Upon his holy throne.

MELODY. C. M.

AARON CHAPIN.

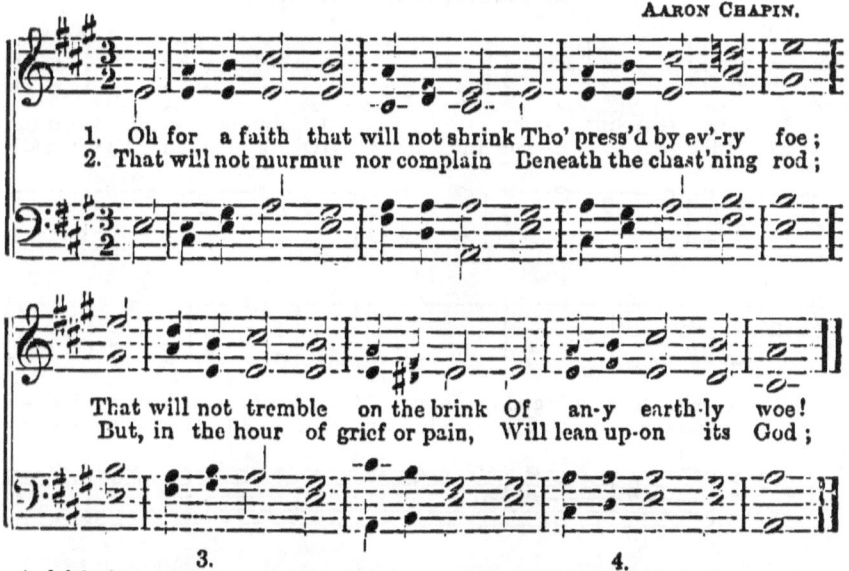

1. Oh for a faith that will not shrink Tho' press'd by ev'-ry foe;
2. That will not murmur nor complain Beneath the chast'ning rod;

That will not tremble on the brink Of an-y earth-ly woe!
But, in the hour of grief or pain, Will lean up-on its God;

3.
A faith that shines more bright and clear
When tempests rage without;
That, when in danger, knows no fear,
In darkness feels no doubt.

4.
A faith that keeps the narrow way
Till life's last hour is fled,
And with a pure and heavenly ray
Lights up a dying bed!

ARLINGTON. C. M.

Dr. Thomas Arne.

1. Jesus! the very tho't of thee With gladness fills my breast;
2. O hope of ev'ry contrite heart, O Joy of all the meek!

But dearer far thy face to see, And in the presence rest.
To those who fall, how kind thou art, How good to those who seek!

3.
And those who find thee, find a bliss
Nor tongue nor pen can show:
The love of Jesus—what it is,
None but his loved ones know.

4.
Jesus, our only joy be thou!
As thou our prize wilt be;
Jesus, be thou our glory now,
And through eternity.

BALERMA. C. M.

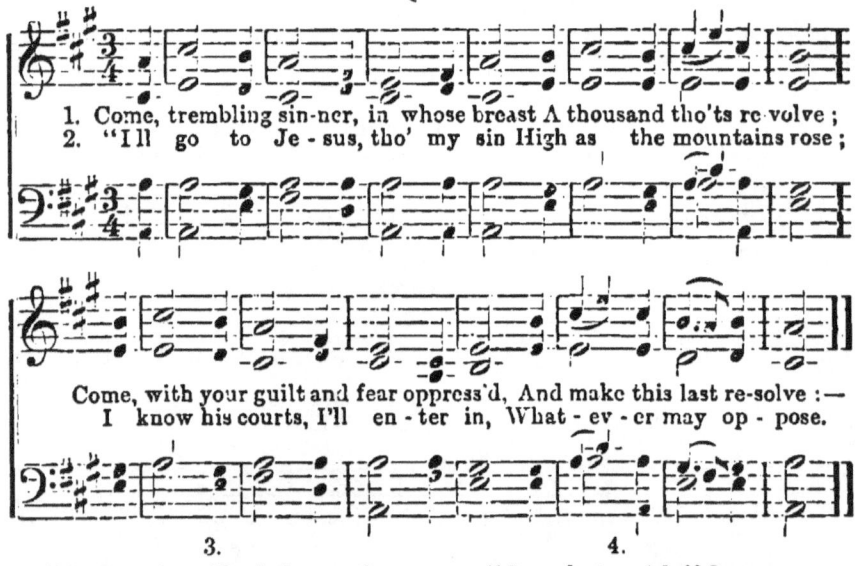

1. Come, trembling sinner, in whose breast A thousand tho'ts revolve
2. "I'll go to Jesus, tho' my sin High as the mountains rose;

Come, with your guilt and fear oppress'd, And make this last resolve:—
I know his courts, I'll enter in, What-ev-er may op-pose.

3.
"Perhaps he will admit my plea,
Perhaps will hear my prayer;
But if I perish, I will pray,
And perish only there.

4.
"I can but perish if I go;
I am resolved to try;
For if I stay away, I know
I must for ever die."

AVON. C. M.

1. Dear Father, to thy mer-cy-seat My soul for shelter flies: 'Tis here I find a safe retreat When storms and tempests rise.

2.
My cheerful hope can never die,
If thou, my God, art near;
Thy grace can raise my comforts high,
And banish every fear.

3.
Oh, never let my soul remove
From this divine retreat!
Still let me trust thy power and love,
And dwell beneath thy feet.

WOODLAND. C. M.

N. D. GOULD.

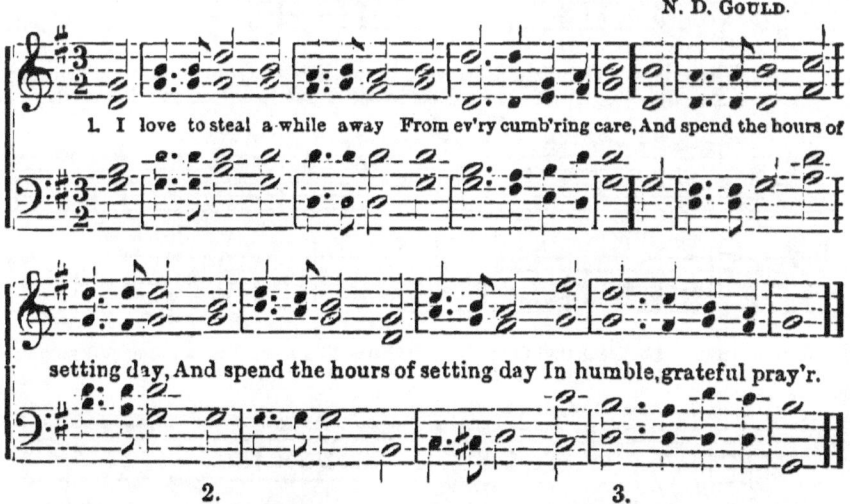

1. I love to steal a while away From ev'ry cumb'ring care, And spend the hours of setting day, And spend the hours of setting day In humble, grateful pray'r.

2.
I love to think on mercies past,
And future good implore;
And all my cares and sorrows cast
On him whom I adore.

3.
Thus, when life's toilsome day is o'er,
May its departing ray
Be calm as this impressive hour,
And lead to endless day!

SPRINGFIELD. C. M. — S. Jackson.

1. Sal-va-tion! O the joy-ful sound! 'Tis mu-sic to our ears; A sove-reign balm for eve-ry wound, A cor-dial for our fears.

2. Salvation! O thou bleeding Lamb!
To thee the praise belongs;
Salvation shall inspire our hearts,
And animate our songs.

3. Salvation! let the echo fly,
The spacious earth around;
While all the armies of the sky
Conspire to raise the sound.

COWPER. C. M. — Dr. L. Mason.

1. There is a fountain fill'd with blood, Drawn from Immanuel's veins; And sinners plunged beneath that flood, Lose all their guilty stains. Lose all their guilty stains.

2. The dy-ing thief re-joiced to see That fountain in his day; And there may I, though vile as he, Wash all my sins away, Wash all my sins a-way.

3. Dear dying Lamb! thy precious blood,
Shall never lose its power.
Till all the ransomed church of God,
Are saved, to sin no more.

4. Since first by faith I saw the stream
Thy flowing wounds supply,
Redeeming love has been my theme,
And shall be, till I die.

CROSS AND CROWN. C. M.

A. CHAPIN.

2.
How happy are the saints above
Who once went sorrowing here;
But now they taste unmingled love,
And joy without a tear.

3.
The consecrated cross I'll bear,
Till death shall set me free,
And then go home my crown to wear,—
For there's a crown for me!

CRESSEY. C. M.

J. H. TENNEY.

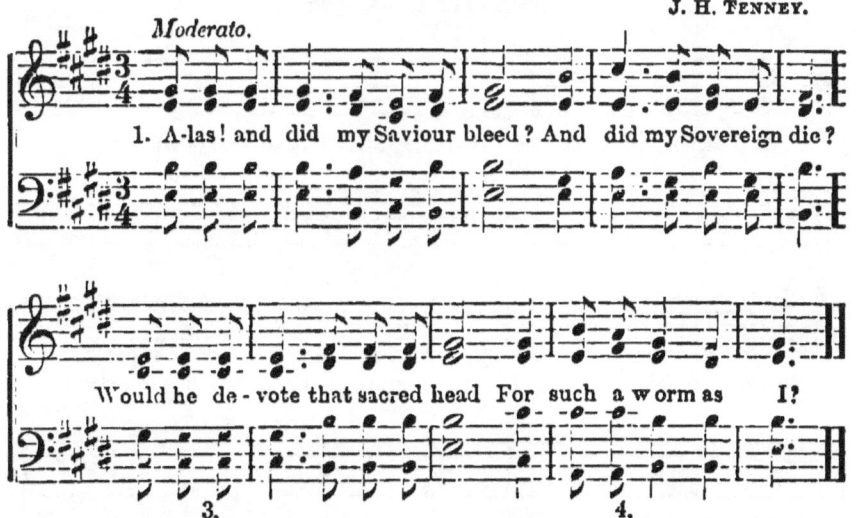

3.
Was it for crimes that I had done,
He groaned upon the tree?
Amazing pity! grace unknown!
And love beyond degree!

4.
But drops of grief can ne'er repay
The debt of love I owe:
Here, Lord, I give myself away;
'Tis all that I can do.

EMMONS. C. M.

1. Thou dear Redeemer, dy-ing Lamb, I love to hear of thee; No music's like thy charming name, Nor half so sweet can be, Nor half so sweet can be.
2. Oh, may I ev-er bear thy voice In mercy to me speak; In thee, my priest, will I re-joice, And thy sal-va-tion seek, And thy sal-va-tion seek.

3.
My Jesus shall be still my theme,
While on this earth I stay;
I'll sing my Jesus' lovely name,
When all things else decay.

4.
When I appear in yonder cloud,
With all his favored throng,
Then will I sing, more sweet, more loud,
And Christ shall be my song.

NAOMI. C. M.

1. Father, whate'er of earthly bliss Thy sovereign will denies, Ac-cept-ed at thy throne of grace, Let this pe-ti-tion rise:

2.
Give me a calm, a thankful heart,
From every murmur free:
The blessings of thy grace impart,
And make me live to thee.

3.
Let the sweet hope that thou art mine
My life and death attend;
Thy presence thro' my journey shine,
And crown my journey's end.

ENON. S. M. 117

D. F. HODGES, by per.

1. Blest be the tie that binds Our hearts in Christian love:
2. Be-fore our Fa-ther's throne We pour our ar-dent pray'rs;

The fel-low-ship of kindred minds Is like to that a-bove.
Our fears, our hopes, our aims are one, Our comforts and our cares.

3.
When we asunder part,
It gives us inward pain;
But we shall still be joined in heart,
And hope to meet again.

4.
From sorrow, toil, and pain,
And sin, we shall be free,
And perfect love and friendship reign
Through all eternity.

BELKNAP. S. M.

MOZART.

1. Sol-diers of Christ a-rise, And put your ar-mor on,—
2. Strong in the Lord of hosts, And in his might-y pow'r:

Strong in the strength which God supplies Thro' his e-ter-nal Son.—
Who in the strength of Je-sus trusts, Is more than con-quer-or.

3.
Stand, then, in his great might,
With all his strength endued;
But take, to arm you for the fight,
The panoply of God:

4.
That, having all things done,
And all your conflicts past,
Ye may o'ercome, thro' Christ alone,
And stand entire at last.

DENNIS. S. M.
NAGELI.

1. My spirit on thy care, Blest Saviour I recline;
Thou wilt not leave me to despair, For thou art love divine.

2. In thee I place my trust; On Thee I calmly rest;
I know thee good, I know thee just, And count thy choice the best.

3. Whate'er events betide,
Thy will they all perform;
Safe in thy breast my head I hide,
Nor fear the coming storm.

4. Let good or ill befall,
It must be good for me,—
Secure of having thee in all,
Of having all in thee.

ST. THOMAS. S. M.
WILLIAMS.

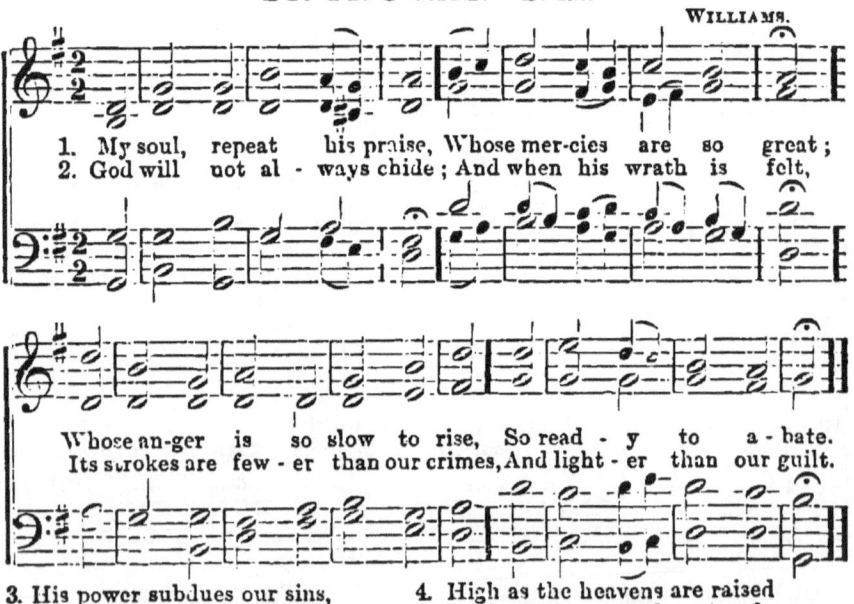

1. My soul, repeat his praise, Whose mercies are so great;
Whose anger is so slow to rise, So ready to abate.

2. God will not always chide; And when his wrath is felt,
Its strokes are fewer than our crimes, And lighter than our guilt.

3. His power subdues our sins,
And his forgiving love,
Far as the east is from the west,
Doth all our guilt remove.

4. High as the heavens are raised
Above the ground we tread,
So far the riches of his grace
Our highest thoughts exceed.

OLMUTZ. S. M.

GREGORIAN.

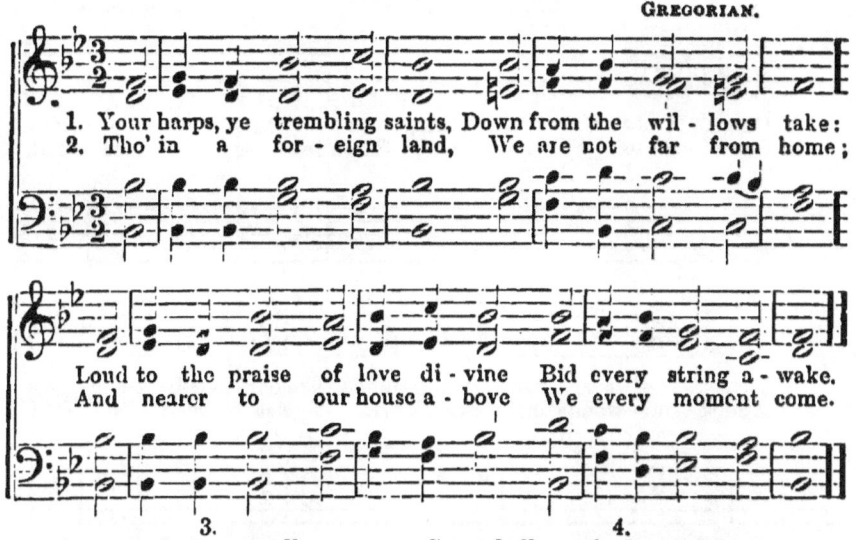

1. Your harps, ye trembling saints, Down from the willows take:
Loud to the praise of love divine Bid every string awake.
2. Tho' in a foreign land, We are not far from home;
And nearer to our house above We every moment come.

3.
When we in darkness walk,
Nor feel the heavenly flame,
Then is the time to trust our God,
And rest upon his name.

4.
Soon shall our doubts and fears
Subside at his control;
His loving-kindness shall break thro'
The midnight of the soul.

LISBON. S. M.

DANIEL REED.

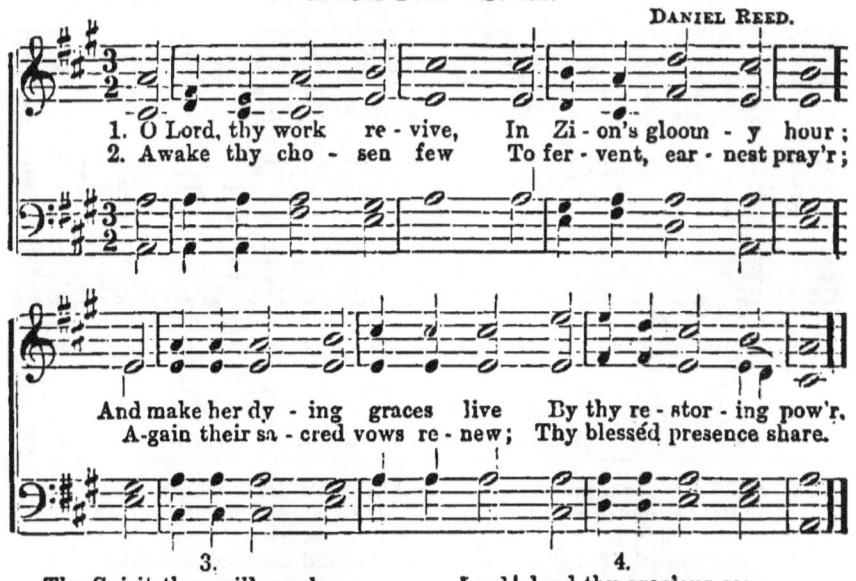

1. O Lord, thy work revive, In Zion's gloomy hour;
And make her dying graces live By thy restoring pow'r.
2. Awake thy chosen few To fervent, earnest pray'r;
Again their sacred vows renew; Thy blessed presence share.

3.
Thy Spirit then will speak
Through lips of feeble clay,
And hearts of adamant will break
And rebels will obey.

4.
Lord! lend thy gracious ear;
Oh, listen to our cry!
Oh, come and bring salvation here!
Our hopes on thee rely.

FAIRMOUNT. S. M.
J. H. TENNEY.

1. Come, Holy Spirit, come, Let thy bright beams arise;
Dispel the sorrow from our minds, The darkness from our eyes.

2. Convince* us of our sin; Then lead to Jesus' blood,
And to our wondering view reveal The secret love of God.

3. 'Tis thine to cleanse the heart,
To sanctify the soul,
To pour fresh life in every part,
And new create the whole.

4. Dwell, Spirit, in our hearts;
Our minds from bondage free;
Then shall we know, and praise, and
The Father, Son, and Thee.   [love.

BOYLSTON. S. M.
DR. L. MASON.

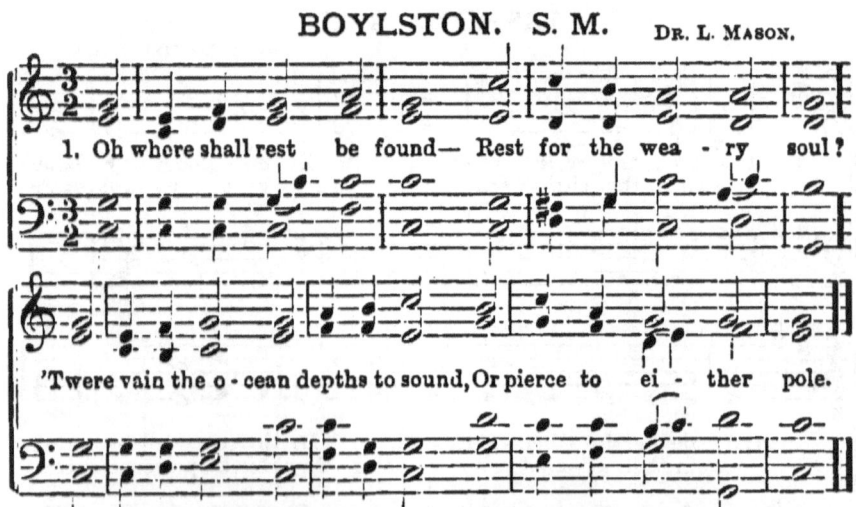

1. Oh where shall rest be found— Rest for the weary soul?
'Twere vain the ocean depths to sound, Or pierce to either pole.

2. The world can never give
The bliss for which we sigh:
'Tis not the whole of life to live,
Nor all of death to die.

3. Beyond this vale of tears
There is a life above,
Unmeasured by the flight of years;
And all that life is love.

4. There is a death whose pang
Outlasts the fleeting breath:
Oh, what eternal horrors hang
Around the second death!

5. Lord God of truth and grace,
Teach us that death to shun;
Lest we be banished from thy face,
And evermore undone.

PLEYEL'S HYMN. 7s.

Pleyel.

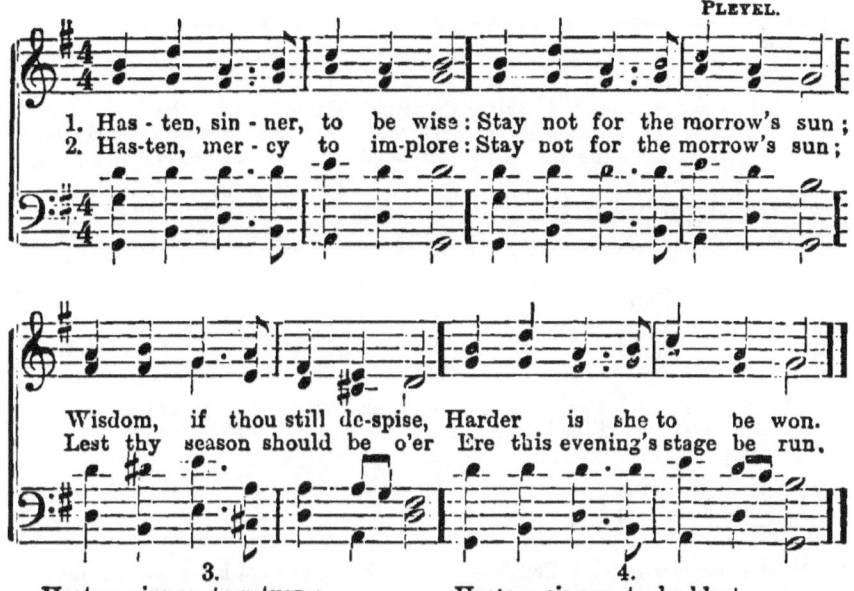

1. Has-ten, sin-ner, to be wise: Stay not for the morrow's sun;
Wisdom, if thou still de-spise, Harder is she to be won.

2. Has-ten, mer-cy to im-plore: Stay not for the morrow's sun;
Lest thy season should be o'er Ere this evening's stage be run.

3.
Hasten, sinner, to return :
Stay not for the morrow's sun,
Lest thy lamp should cease to burn
Ere salvation's work is done.

4.
Hasten, sinner, to be blest :
Stay not for the morrow's sun ;
Lest the curse should thee arrest
Ere the morrow is begun.

WILMOT. 8s & 7s.

C. M. von Weber.

1. Je-sus, hail! enthron'd in glo-ry, There for-ev-er to a-bide;
All the heavenly hosts a-dore thee, Seated at thy Father's side.

2.
There for sinners thou art pleading,
There thou dost our place prepare ;
Ever for us interceding,
Till in glory we appear.

3.
Worship, honor, power, and blessing,
Thou art worthy to receive ;
Loudest praises, without ceasing,
Meet it is for us to give.

MARTYN. 7s.

MARSH.

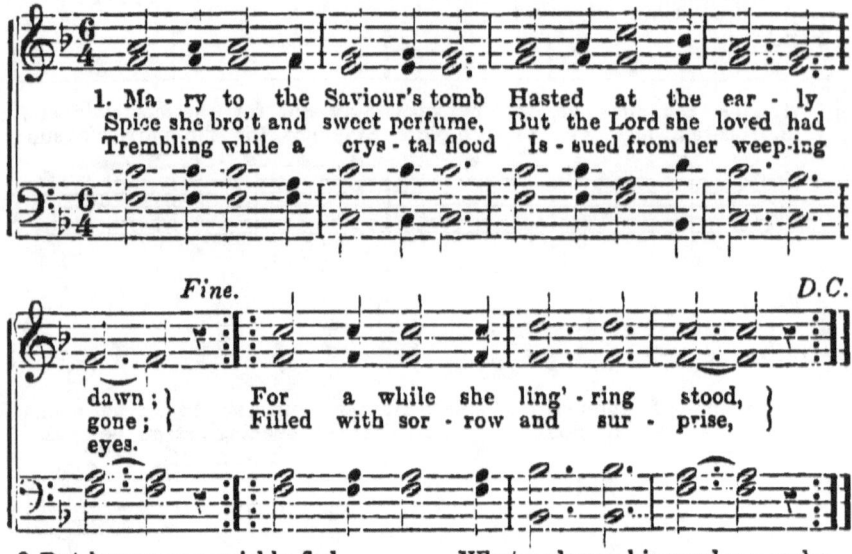

1. Ma-ry to the Saviour's tomb Hasted at the ear-ly dawn;
Spice she bro't and sweet perfume, But the Lord she loved had gone;
Trembling while a crys-tal flood Is-sued from her weep-ing eyes.
For a while she ling'-ring stood,
Filled with sor-row and sur-prise,

2. But her sorrow quickly fled,
When she heard his welcome voice,
Christ had risen from the dead ;
Now he bids her heart rejoice :
What a change his word can make,
Turning darkness into day!
Ye who weep for Jesus' sake,
He will wipe your tears away.

GREENVILLE. 8s & 7s.

ROUSSEAU.

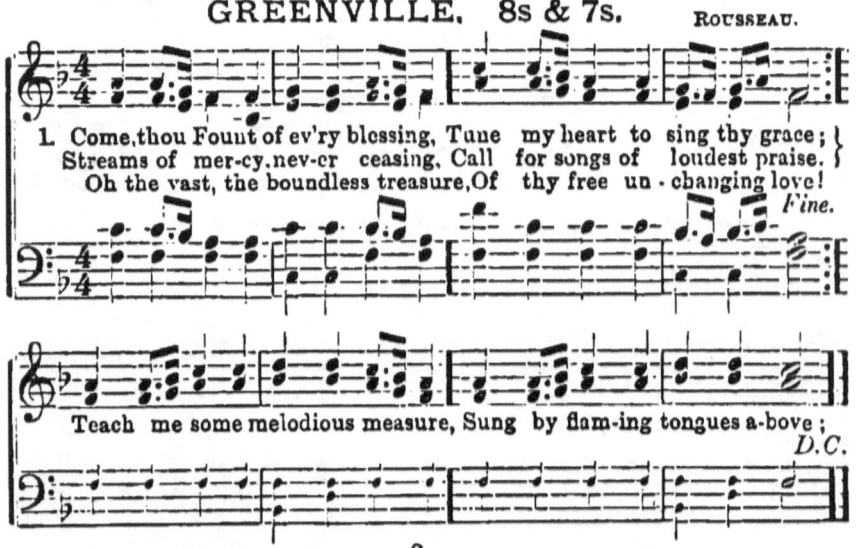

1. Come, thou Fount of ev'ry blessing, Tune my heart to sing thy grace;
Streams of mer-cy, nev-er ceasing, Call for songs of loudest praise.
Oh the vast, the boundless treasure, Of thy free un-changing love!
Teach me some melodious measure, Sung by flam-ing tongues a-bove;

2.
Jesus sought me when a stranger,
Wandering from the fold of God ;
He to rescue me from danger,
Interposed his precious blood.
Oh, to grace how great a debtor
Daily I'm constrained to be!
Let thy goodness, like a fetter,
Bind my wandering heart to thee.

TOPLADY. 7s. Dr. T. Hastings. 123

1. Rock of Ages! cleft for me; Let me hide myself in thee!
D. C.—Be of sin the double cure—Cleanse me from its guilt and pow'r.

Let the wa-ter and the blood, From thy riv-en side which flow'd,

2.
Could my zeal no respite know,
Could my tears forever flow—
All for sin could not atone:
Thou must save, and thou alone!
Nothing in my hand I bring;
Simply to thy cross I cling.

3.
While I draw this fleeting breath,
When my eyelids close in death,
When I soar to worlds unknown,
See thee on thy judgment throne,—
Rock of Ages! cleft for me,
Let me hide myself in thee!

LINCOLN. 7s. E. Roberts, by per.

1. Je-sus, lov-er of my soul, Let me to thy bosom fly,
While the raging billows roll, While the tempest still is high;
D. C. Safe in-to the haven guide, Oh, re-ceive my soul at last.

Hide me, O my Saviour, hide, Till the storm of life is past:

2. Other refuge have I none;
   Hangs my helpless soul on thee:
   Leave, ah, leave me not alone!
   Still support and comfort me;
   All my trust on thee is stay'd;
   All my help from thee I bring;
   Cover my defenceless head
   With the shadow of thy wing.

3. Thou O Christ, art all I want,
   Boundless love in thee I find,
   Raise the fallen, cheer the faint,
   Heal the sick, and lead the blind.
   Just and holy is thy name,
   I am all unrighteous;
   Vile and full of sin I am—
   Thou art full of truth and grace.

MISSIONARY HYMN. 7s & 6s.

Dr. L. Mason.

1. From Greenland's i-cy mountains, From India's cor-al strand; Where Afric's sunny fountains Roll down their golden sand; From many an ancient riv-er, From many a palm-y plain, They call us to de-liv-er Their land from error's chain.

2. What tho' the spi-cy breez-es, Blow soft o'er Ceylon's isle, Though ev'-ry prospect pleas-es, And only man is vile? In vain with lav-ish kind-ness The gifts of God are strown; The heathen, in his blindness, Bows down to wood and stone.

3.
Shall we, whose souls are lighted
  With wisdom from on high,
Shall we to men benighted
  The lamp of life deny?
Salvation! oh, salvation!
  The joyful sound proclaim,
Till earth's remotest nation
  Has learn'd Messiah's name.

4.
Waft, waft, ye winds, His story;
  And you, ye waters, roll,
Till, like a sea of glory,
  It spreads from pole to pole;
Till o'er our ransom'd nature
  The Lamb for sinners slain,
Redeemer, King, Creator,
  In bliss returns to reign.

OLIVET. 6s & 4s.

RAY PALMER. DR. L. MASON.

1. My faith looks up to thee, Thou Lamb of Calvary, Saviour divine! Now hear me while I pray: Take all my guilt a-way: Oh, let me, from this day, Be wholly thine.
2. May thy rich grace impart Strength to my failing heart, My zeal inspire! As thou hast died for me, Oh, may my love to thee Pure, warm, and changeless be, A living fire!

3. While life's dark maze I tread,
  And griefs around me spread,
  Be thou my guide;
  Bid darkness turn to day,
  Wipe sorrow's tears away,
  Nor let me ever stray
  From thee aside,

4. When ends life's transient dream,
  When death's cold, sullen stream
  Shall o'er me roll,
  Blest Saviour! then, in love,
  Fear and distrust remove;
  Oh, bear me safe above—
  A ransomed soul!

AMERICA. 6s & 4s.

HANDEL.

1. My country, 'tis of thee, Sweet land of lib-er-ty, Of thee I sing; Land where my fathers died, Land of the pilgrim's pride, From every mountain side Let freedom ring.
2. My na-tive country, thee, Land of the noble free, Thy name I love; I love thy rocks and rills, Thy woods and templed hills, My heart with rapture thrills Like that above.

3. Let music swell the breeze,
  And ring from all the trees
  Sweet freedom's song;
  Let mortal tongues awake,
  Let all that breathe partake,
  Let rocks their silence break,
  The sound prolong.

4. Our Father's God! to thee,
  Author of liberty!
  To thee we sing;
  Long may our land be bright
  With freedom's holy light,
  Protect us by thy might,
  Great God, our King.

MAXIM.

2.
Look, how we grovel here below,
Fond of these trifling toys!
Our souls can neither fly nor go
To reach eternal joys.

3.
In vain we tune our formal songs;
In vain we strive to rise:
Hosannas languish on our tongues,
And our devotion dies.

INDEX

Titles in CAPITALS; first lines in Roman.

Title	PAGE		Title	PAGE
A few more years shall roll	12		FAIRMOUNT	120
AFTER TOIL COMETH REST	42		FAITH	19
Alas! and did my Saviour bleed	115		Father, whate'er of earthly bliss	116
All glory to Jesus is given	28		FEDERAL STREET	102
All hail the power of Jesus' name	109		From every stormy wind that blows	104
AMERICA	125		From Greenland's icy mountains	124
Amid the toil and pain of life	92		GENTLY LEAD US	63
Arise, ye people, and adore	107		Gently, Lord, O gently lead us	63
ARLINGTON	112		GERALD	99
AT THE DOOR	64		GLAD TIDINGS	69
AVON	113		Go and tell Jesus all thy sin	29
BALERMA	112		God is the refuge of his saints	104
Bathed in unfailing sunlight	96		GOING HOME	33
BEAUTIFUL RIVER	25		GO TO JESUS	31
Behold a stranger at the door	103		GREENVILLE	122
BEHOLD THE LAMB OF GOD	35		Happy the heart where graces reign	110
BELKNAP	117		HAMBURG	101
BE NOT DISCOURAGED	94		Hark, sinner, while God from on high	67
Beside the throne of God	77		Hark! the choral band	10
BEYOND THE SWELLING FLOOD	24		HARK! 'TIS THE WATCHMAN'S CRY	23
Blest be the tie that binds	117		Hasten, sinner, to be wise	121
Blest be thy love, dear Lord	93		Have you heard of the golden paved city	46
BOYLSTON	120		HEBRON	102
Broad is the road that leads to death	105		HE CALLETH THEE	29
BY THE JASPER SEA	58		HE CARETH FOR THEE	97
CALL TO PRAISE	71		HOME OF THE BLEST	37
Careworn trav'ler on life's ocean	91		Hosanna! be our cheerful song	109
CHRIST THE REFUGE	90		HOSANNA TO OUR KING	73
CLING CLOSE TO THE ROCK	15		I AM WAITING BY THE RIVER	14
CLINGING TO THE CROSS	36		I AM VERY HAPPY	78
Come hither, all ye weary souls	102		I gave my life for thee	72
Come, Holy Spirit, come	120		I have entered the valley of blessing	7
Come, Holy Spirit, Heavenly Dove	126		I know there are homes up above	42
Come, let us Praise the Saviour's name	71		I love to steal awhile away	113
Come, thou fount of every blessing	122		I LOVE TO TELL THE STORY	20
Come, trembling sinner, in whose breast	112		I love to think of that happy land	58
COME TO JESUS	81		In some way or other the Lord will provide	57
COME TO ME, SAVIOUR	33		In those beautiful mansions	22
COME TO THE SAVIOUR	34		IT IS I	5
COME UNTO ME	43, 49		JEHOVAH JIREH	57
COMING TO JESUS	13		Jesus, hail! enthroned in glory	121
CORONATION	109		Jesus, I am never weary	70
COURAGE! FELLOW PILGRIM	11		JESUS IS MIGHTY TO SAVE	28
COWPER	114		Jesus, lover of my soul	123
CRESSEY	115		Jesus, my all, to heaven is gone	98
CROSS AND CROWN	115		JESUS PAID IT ALL	85
Dear Father, to thy mercy seat	113		Jesus the very tho't of thee	112
Dear Redeemer, only Thee	4		JESUS WILL GATHER US HOME	89
DEDHAM	110		JOYFUL BE THE HOURS	3
DENNIS	118		JUST AS I AM	95
DRESDEN	9		KEEP ON PRAYING	60
DUANE STREET	98		LET US PASS OVER THE RIVER	74
DUKE STREET	101		Life is the time to serve the Lord	105
DUNDEE	107		LIGHTS ALONG THE SHORE	50
EMMONS	116		LINCOLN	123
ENON	117		LISBON	110
EVEN ME	50		Long my spirit pined in sorrow	60
Faint, pursuing, on we go	86		Lord, I am thine	103
FAINT, YET PURSUING	86		Lord, I hear the showers of blessing	59

INDEX.

Title	Page
Lord, to thee in deep contrition	9
Majestic sweetness sits enthroned	108
MARLOW	103
MARTYN	122
Mary to the Saviour's tomb	122
MEAR	111
MELODY	111
MIDST SORROW AND CARE	39
MISSIONARY HYMN	124
Must Jesus bear the cross alone	115
My country, 'tis of thee	125
My faith looks up to thee	125
My heavenly home is bright and fair	33
My Jesus as thou wilt	53
My Saviour stands waiting	64
My soul, repeat his praise	118
My spirit on thy care	118
MY SWEET HOME IN HEAVEN	92
NAOMI	116
Nought of merit or of price	85
NEARER HOME	8
NEARER, MY GOD, TO THEE	21, 99
Nearer my home in heaven	66
Nearing the better land	91
NOTHING BUT LEAVES	82
Now to the Lord a noble song	101
O come guilty sinner	63
O city of the jasper wall	84
O'er the hill the sun is setting	3
O Father, let me bear the cross	35
O for a faith that will not shrink	111
OH HOW HE LOVES	40
Oh help us Lord! each hour of need	107
Oh Lord, thy work revive	119
Oh that my load of sin were gone	106
Oh where shall rest be found	120
OLIVET	125
OLMUTZ	119
O may I bring Jesus my sorrow	18
One sweetly solemn tho't	66
ONLY REMEMBERED	83
ONLY THEE	4
ONWARD, CHRISTIAN SOLDIERS	20
Onward we'er travelling here below	83
Oppres'd with noonday's scorching heat	6
ORTONVILLE	108
O the fields are ripe for harvest	47
O the love of Christ	76
OVER THERE	41
O when shall I dwell	37
PERRIN	51
PETERBORO'	110
PLEYEL'S HYMN	121
RETREAT	104
ROCKINGHAM	103
Rock of Ages	123
ROSCOE	106
Salvation! O the joyful sound	114
Saviour! I follow on	19
SCARBOROUGH	107
SECURITY	93
SESSIONS	103
Shall we gather at the river	25
SHALL WE KNOW EACH OTHER	44
Shall we meet beyond the river	83
Sing, ye redeemed of the Lord	108
SINNER, COME	65
Sinner, so thoughtless	52
Soldiers of Christ, arise	117
Speed thee with the message	69
SPRINGFIELD	114
STAND UP FOR JESUS	16
STAND UP FOR JESUS ALWAYS	17
ST. THOMAS	118
SWEET BY-AND-BY	26
Sweet was the time when first I felt	110
Tell me the old, old story	32
THE BETTER LAND	10
THE BRIGHT FOREVER	83
THE CELESTIAL COUNTRY	13
THE ETERNAL CITY	46
The gentle, holy Jesus	35
THE HALLOWED SPOT	30
THE HARVEST IS PASSING	67
THE LAND CELESTIAL	62
THE LAND OF BLISS	84
The Lord descended from above	111
THE LORD WILL PROVIDE	57
THE LOVE OF CHRIST	76
THE NEW JERUSALEM	56
THE OLD, OLD STORY	32
THE PARADISE HOME	87
THE PERFECT REST	70
THE PILGRIM'S SONG	12
There are lights by the shore	50
There is a fountain	114
There is a land celestial	62
There is a safe and secret place	51, 97
There is a spot to me more dear	30
There's a band of angel watchers	41
There's a friend above all others	40
THERE'S ROOM FOR ALL	22
THERE'S SOMETHING TO DO	56
THE SHADOW OF THE CROSS	6
The sands of time are sinking	13
THE SUNNY SHORE	48
THE VALLEY OF BLESSING	7
THE VOICE OF MERCY	52
THE WATER OF LIFE	77
THE WAY	75
THE WAY IS DARK	75
They have reached the sunny shore	48
THIS I DID FOR THEE	72
THY WILL BE DONE	53
Thou dear Redeemer	116
Thus far the Lord has lead	102
To-day the Saviour calls	45
TOPLADY	123
TOURJEE	106
Tossing in dreamy sleep	90
TURNER	126
Up and away	88
UNITY	100
Voyager o'er life's rough tide	97
Wand'ring afar from the dwellings	79
WARD	104
We are walking by faith	26
We are journeying home	87
WELLS	105
We're trav'ling home	61
When Jesus left the throne	73
When our work is ended	74
When we cross the crystal river	54
When we hear the music	44
When shall we meet again	100
When I survey the wondrous cross	101
WHERE ARE THE NINE	79
Who will gather the grain	47
Why stand ye here idle	56
WILL YOU GO	61
WINDHAM	105
With all my powers of heart	106
WILMOT	121
WILL YOU GO TO CHRIST	68
WOODLAND	113
Yes, we shall meet	24
Your harps, ye trembling saints	119

A. B. KIDDER & SON'S MUSIC TYPOGRAPHY.

www.ingramcontent.com/pod-product-compliance
Lightning Source LLC
Chambersburg PA
CBHW020113170426
43199CB00009B/510